www.wadsworth.com

wadsworth.com is the World Wide Web site for Wadsworth and is your direct source to dozens of online resources.

At *wadsworth.com* you can find out about supplements, demonstration software, and student resources. You can also send email to many of our authors and preview new publications and exciting new technologies.

wadsworth.com
Changing the way the world learns®

SIXTH EDITION

Writing Papers in Psychology

A STUDENT GUIDE TO RESEARCH REPORTS, ESSAYS, PROPOSALS, POSTERS, AND BRIEF REPORTS

Ralph L. Rosnow *and* **Mimi Rosnow**

THOMSON
━━━━━✦━━━━━ ™
WADSWORTH

Australia • Canada • Mexico • Singapore • Spain
United Kingdom • United States

THOMSON
✳
WADSWORTH

Publisher: Victoria J. Knight
Assistant Editor: Jennifer Wilkinson
Editorial Assistant: Monica Sarmiento
Marketing Manager: Kathleen Morgan
Marketing Assistant: Lauren Anderson
Advertising Project Manager: Shemika
Britt
Project Manager, Editorial Production:
Stephanie Zunich
Print Buyer: Kristine Waller

Permissions Editor: Sue Ewing
Production Service: Robin Gold,
Forbes Mill Press
Text Designer: Robin Gold
Copy Editor: Margaret Ritchie
Cover Designer: Rokusek Design
Cover Image: Rokusek Design
Compositor: Linda Weidemann,
Wolf Creek Press
Printer: Webcom Limited

For more information about our
products, contact us at:
Thomson Learning
Academic Resource Center
1-800-423-0563
For permission to use material
from this text, contact us by:
Phone: 1-800-730-2214
Fax: 1-800-730-2215
Web: http://www.thomsonrights.com

Wadsworth/Thomson Learning
10 Davis Drive
Belmont, CA 94002-3098
USA

Asia
Thomson Learning
5 Shenton Way #01-01
UIC Building
Singapore 068808

Australia
Nelson Thomson Learning
102 Dodds Street
South Melbourne, Victoria 3205
Australia

Canada
Nelson Thomson Learning
1120 Birchmount Road
Toronto, Ontario M1K 5G4
Canada

Europe/Middle East/Africa
Thomson Learning
High Holborn House
50/51 Bedford Row
London WC1R 4LR
United Kingdom

Library of Congress Control Number:
2002104450

ISBN 0-534-52395-1

To the partnership
that brought this book about

and

to Miles and R.J.
whose promise shines

Contents

Exhibits

Preface for Instructors

Writing Papers in Psychology began as a handout designed to help students write research reports back in the days when word processors were called typewriters. The first edition of this book was, in fact, composed on a typewriter; it was not until the third edition that the picture on the cover hinted of a computer keyboard. Typewriters are artifacts of an earlier generation, and in this sixth edition, we emphasize advances within the grasp of this generation of students. Guided by the following flowchart, students writing research reports, essays, proposals, posters, and brief reports as handouts can refer to specific chapters and selections as needed:

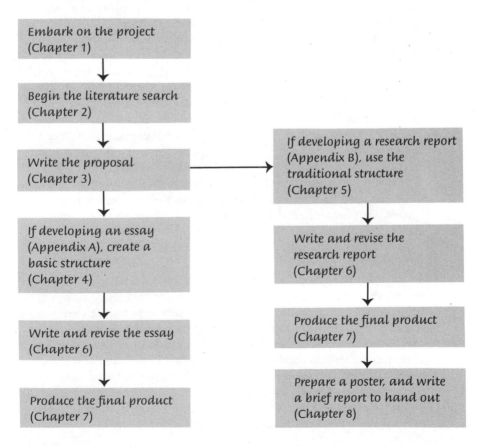

Recommended Style

The recommended style of presentation of student essays and research reports in *Writing Papers* is in the spirit of the fifth edition of the *Publication Manual of the American Psychological Association* (hereafter called the APA manual), published by the APA in 2001. Among the changes in the APA manual are certain emphases on the reporting of statistical results, which reflect repeated reminders in recent years of the failings and limitations of the rhetoric of the "accept/reject" paradigm in null hypothesis significance testing. In 1999, the APA's Task Force on Statistical Inference proposed guidelines for addressing this situation, including the reporting of interval estimates for effect sizes involving principal outcomes and paying heed to statistical power considerations in significance testing. The sample research report in Appendix B has been revised to embrace these recommendations.

There are inconsistencies in the APA manual's discussion of statistical topics, however, which could be a source of confusion to psychology students:

♦ For example, in discussing "Notes to a Table," the APA manual recommends the use of "asterisks for the two-tailed p values and an alternate symbol (e.g., daggers) for the one-tailed p values" (p. 171). However, an example on the same page shows asterisks being used for p values of F distributions, although such p values are naturally one-tailed. If a student believed that the asterisked p value meant it was two-tailed and, having predicted the direction of the result, naively divided the p value by 2, the new p value of F would be not "one tailed" but "one-half-tailed."

♦ The APA manual properly cautions against the reporting of "multiple degree-of-freedom effect indicators" (p. 26) but then illustrates an ANOVA table (p. 162) in which six out of seven effect sizes are multiple degree-of-freedom indicators based on omnibus F tests. The rule of thumb used in *Writing Papers* is to report effect sizes only in association with focused statistical tests (e.g., F tests with numerator $df = 1$, any t test, or any 1-df chi-square), but never in association with omnibus tests (e.g., F tests with numerator $df > 1$ or chi-square with $df > 1$).

♦ As regards the appropriate effect size indicator, the APA manual recommends Cohen's d but fails to mention either Hedges's g or the Pearson r, which are also quite suitable in the simple setting of two groups. An advantage of the r statistic is that it is serviceable when t, F, or z contrasts are used to address a focused question in research designs with more than two conditions, as illustrated in the sample research report. The APA manual also recommends certain squared indices (i.e., r^2, η^2, ω^2, R^2, ϕ^2), all of which, regrettably, are susceptible to the expository problem that small, but sometimes very meaningful, effects may appear to essentially disappear when squared.

Thus, although the APA manual is largely without peer in most other respects, problems such as these are one reason why we say that *Writing Papers* is "in the spirit" of the APA manual rather than matching it exactly.

Another reason is that the APA manual is focused on the preparation of manuscripts for submission to journals, whereas only an infinitesimally small number of undergraduate essays or research reports are revised for submission to journal editors. Student papers are written for instructors to evaluate and grade, and it makes sense that the needs of instructors are different in some ways from journal editors' and reviewers' requirements. For example, many instructors of research courses like to see the raw data and possibly even the statistical calculations. Thus, the sample research report contains an appendix for this information, so that instructors can more easily assess whether any mistakes are due to misunderstanding, carelessness, or typographical errors. Another departure from the APA manual is the cover page of the student's paper, because there is no compelling reason to require a "running head" (the purpose of which is to suggest to the copyeditor an abbreviated title to be printed at the top of the pages of a published article), but there is good reason to ask for a page header and for identifying information relevant to the course and the instructor.

In fact, the APA has for some time been flexible in many of its stylistic requirements, as indicated by various responses to questions appearing on the old APA Publication Manual Web site (www.apa.org/journals/faq.html). For example, a student asked whether the title shown on the title page of a manuscript belonged in the middle of the page or closer to the top of the page, because the student had noticed that "colleagues' versions of the Publication Manual showed a different graphic for the title page of a manuscript." The APA's response was that either version was correct.

Another writer, who was also using the fourth edition of the APA manual, asked why underlining was required instead of italicizing, because a word processor makes it just as easy to italicize as underline. The APA's answer was that underlining signals to the typesetter to use italics, but that if a manuscript for publication was in final form, it was acceptable to use the italicizing function to mimic what would be typeset in italics and to improve the appearance of the manuscript. The fifth edition of the APA manual prefers that italics rather than underlining be used, but even when italicizing is used in a manuscript accepted for publication, the copyeditor generally inserts an underline anyway.

Regarding the hanging versus paragraph-type indent used when formatting references, on which the APA manual has wavered back and forth in the third, fourth, and fifth editions, the APA's Web site response to a question about this practice was "If you are preparing a manuscript in final form, meaning that the manuscript will not later be typeset and published, you may prefer to format references with a hanging indent to enhance readability." The fifth edition of the APA manual recommends, but does not insist on, the methods texts in psychology still pay scant (if any) attention to effect size estimation, the actual assessment of statistical power, and other basic issues emphasized by the APA Task Force on Statistical Inference.

All stylistic requirements in the APA manual can be easily accomplished with any word-processing program. This book was composed on Windows 98 and Microsoft Word 2000, but one of us prefers Mac OS and Appleworks. The APA has a software product called *APA-Style Helper 3.0*, which is compatible with Microsoft Word or WordPerfect, using Windows or Mac OS. In our recent experience, however, we found *APA-Style Helper 3* more cumbersome to use than a general word-processing program. The world that most college students enter after they graduate is rarely ruled by strict APA style guidelines. For experienced writers, who are likely to submit their work to a wide variety of journals, we recommend *EndNote,* a software program that can be used with Microsoft Word or WordPerfect to instantaneously format references in any standardized style (including the APA style).

Acknowledgments

We thank two outstanding psychology teachers, Anne A. Skleder (Alvernia College) and Bruce Rind (Temple University), for early versions of the sample papers, which we have reworked in different editions of *Writing Papers*. We thank MaryLu Rosenthal for advising us through the previous editions about the methods and means available for a literature search in a modern college library. We thank Linda Beebe and Carolyn Gosling of the American Psychological Association for information enabling us to update our discussion of PsycINFO. We thank Eric K. Foster for allowing us to look over his shoulder in Chapter Two. We benefited from reference resources at Temple University's Paley Library, particularly the superb Web site for psychology students that was created by Richard Lezenby. We are grateful to Vicki Knight of Wadsworth Press for her continued interest and enthusiasm, to Ken King for encouraging us to get started on this book many years ago, and to James Brace-Thompson for his support of previous editions. Once again, we thank Margaret Ritchie for her skillful editing.

We thank the following colleagues, whose helpful suggestions have improved one or more editions of *Writing Papers:*

John B. Best, Eastern Illinois University
Thomas Brown, Utica College of Syracuse University
David E. Campbell, Humboldt State University
Scott D. Churchill, University of Dallas
Nicholas DiFonzo, Rochester Institute of Technology
Nancy Eldred, San Jose State University
Ken Elliott, University of Maine at Augusta
Robert Gallen, Georgetown College
David Goldstein, Duke University

John Hall, Texas Wesleyan University
James W. Kalat, North Carolina State University
Allan J. Kimmel, Groupe École Supérieure de Commerce de Paris, France
Arlene Lundquist, Mount Union College
Joann Montepare, Tufts University
Quentin Newhouse, Jr., Bowie State University
Arthur Nonneman, Asbury College
Edgar O'Neal, Tulane University
Rick Pollack, Merrimack College
Maureen Powers, Vanderbilt University
Robert Rosenthal, University of California at Riverside
Gordon W. Russell, University of Lethbridge, Canada
Helen Shoemaker, California State University at Hayward
John Sparrow, State University of New York at Geneseo
David B. Strohmetz, Monmouth University
Stephen A. Truhon, Winston-Salem State University

Finally, we thank the many users of *Writing Papers*. Your comments and suggestions have helped us to improve each new edition. We again invite instructors and students to send us comments and suggestions for further improvements.

Ralph and Mimi Rosnow

1

GETTING STARTED

Writing papers to fulfill course requirements means knowing what the instructor expects and then formulating a plan to accomplish your goal on schedule. This chapter includes some simple dos and don'ts to help you avoid pitfalls and to ensure that the assignment will be completed on time and that it will represent your best work.

Where to Begin

There was once an intriguing character named Joe Gould, who, after graduating from Harvard in 1911 and trying his hand at a number of futile endeavors, moved to New York and began to hang around Greenwich Village coffee shops. He told people that he had mastered the language of seagulls, and in fact, he did an uncanny imitation of one. He was best known, however, for an ambitious project he claimed to be compiling, called the "Oral History of Our Times." He boasted of having accumulated a stack of notebooks that stood 7 feet tall, and he carried brown paper bags with him that, he said, contained research notes.

Joe Gould died in a psychiatric hospital while doing his seagull imitation. Some years later, in a profile article written by Joseph Mitchell for the *New Yorker* magazine, it was revealed that Joe Gould never started his "Oral History," his notebooks were a myth, and his brown bags merely contained other bags and yellowed newspaper clippings. For students with required writing assignments, Joe Gould is a metaphor for the most challenging aspect of any project: how to get started.

To begin your project, you need some clear objectives. Here is a checklist of questions to focus your approach:

- ◆ What is the purpose of the required assignment?
- ◆ Do I choose the theme or topic, or will it be assigned by the instructor?

- How long should the paper be?
- Will interim papers (for example, a proposal and progress reports) be required, and when are they due?
- When is the final report due, and how does this date mesh with my other assignments (for example, exams and other papers)?

You can talk with other students about their impressions, but the person who knows *exactly* what is expected of you is the instructor. Before you turn on a word processor or sharpen any pencils, meet with the instructor, articulate what you understand the assignment to be, and ask if your understanding is accurate. One instructor wrote to us that many of his students were reluctant to take this initial step, even though they hadn't a clue about a topic for an assigned paper. But those who did come in, even without an idea for a topic, benefited from a meeting and, in most cases, went away with at least the beginning of a direction for their papers.

Focusing on Your Objective

Once you have a topic, thinking through the assignment will sharpen your intellectual process. To help you focus on your particular objective, it is well to understand the differences between the essay and the research report and the different varieties of each of these forms. We suggest you pause at this point and read the sample essay (Appendix A) and the sample research report (Appendix B) at the end of this book, as we will be referring to them repeatedly. If you are writing a senior thesis or a master's thesis, your paper will probably contain features of essays *and* research reports. Let us start with the general differences between the essay and the research report (see Exhibit 1), so you can concentrate your efforts on whichever project you have been assigned.

One distinction highlighted in Exhibit 1 is that a literature search usually forms the core of the essay, whereas empirical data form the core of the research report. The literature search for the research report typically involves a few key studies that serve as theoretical starting points, so you can expect to

EXHIBIT 1 Differences between essays and research reports

Essay	Research Report
1. Is based on literature search; no hard data of your own to interpret	1. Is based on data that you have collected; literature search involving only a few key studies
2. Is structured by you to fit your particular topic	2. Is structured to follow a traditional form
3. Puts ideas into the context of a particular thesis	3. Reports your own research findings to others

spend more time in the library if you are writing an essay. Of course, you still must spend time in the library if you are writing a research report, because you will need to read articles and books that are merely abstracted in the records you retrieved online. You will also find it useful to peruse recent encyclopedias of psychology and other general reference works in the stacks (the shelves throughout the library). If you are writing an undergraduate thesis or a master's thesis, you will be expected to do a thorough search of the relevant literature. We will show how in the next chapter.

A second distinction is that the composition of the essay, although somewhat formal, is more flexible than that of the research report, which has a much more standardized structure. The structure of an essay needs to be flexible because there are different types of essays that represent quite different objectives. Furthermore, it is not always evident, even to very experienced writers, how a final manuscript will take shape until they have actually had an opportunity to think about everything in more than just a piecemeal fashion. Instructors expect the structure of the research report to conform to a general tradition that has evolved over many years. As a consequence, research reports typically include an abstract, an introduction, a method section, a results section, a discussion of the results, and a list of the references cited.

The final distinction noted in Exhibit 1 is that the essay puts issues and ideas into the context of a particular theme or thesis, whereas the objective of the research report is to describe your empirical investigation to others. The theme in a research report usually involves testable hypotheses. What you found in your research must be put into the context of these hypotheses, but not by the same approach you use when writing an essay. We will have more to say about this last point later.

Three Types of Essays

If this were a course in the English department, you would be taught about three types of essays: the expository essay, the argumentative essay, and the case study. Each has its own objective. In psychology courses, however, student essays are often expected to have some characteristics of more than just one type. For example, John Smith's sample essay in Appendix A has at least a flavor of all three types, although it is primarily an expository essay.

First, the objective of an *expository essay* is to inform the reader in depth on a specific topic or theme—in John Smith's case, two views of intelligence. The word *expository* means "expounding," "setting forth," or "explaining." Expository essays call for accessibility in writing, like the articles that are in the science sections of top newspapers (for example, in the science section of the *New York Times* each Tuesday), but in more detail and with full citations. John does not begin by writing, "I am going to explain two views of intelligence." That is, in fact, his aim (implicit in the title of his paper), but his opening paragraph shows elegance and artistry as he draws the reader into the exposition. Other examples of expository essays in undergraduate psychology courses might be "Similarities and Differences Between Operant and Classical Conditioning" and "The Role of Teachers' Expectations in Students' Academic Performance." Each title promises to inform the reader about some topic in detail.

Second, the objective of persuading the reader to accept a particular point of view calls for an *argumentative essay*. In John Smith's paper, there is an implicit argument for what he terms the "multiplex approach." Another example of this type of essay in psychology might be one that argued the cost-effectiveness of behavior therapy as opposed to a more time-consuming psychotherapeutic approach. In psychology courses, argumentative essays usually attempt either to advance or to challenge the applicability of some position or theoretical idea to a realm beyond the one it was intended for. Such essays ask readers either to form a new view or to change their minds about a particular theoretical idea. If you are writing a primarily argumentative essay, be sure to express all viewpoints fairly, and not just in a "take it or leave it" fashion. Show that you recognize gray areas as you develop your position, and present documentation to support it. If you are arguing against a particular viewpoint, you can collect specific quotations to illustrate that you have represented it accurately. Otherwise, you might be accused of making a "straw man argument," which means that, to buttress your own view, you represented the other side in a false, unfair, or misleading way. Before you begin to write, it is usually a good idea to argue your point of view with someone who is a good listener and who promises to be critical. Jot down questions and counterarguments while they are fresh in your mind so that you can deal with them in your paper.

Third, the goal of the *descriptive essay* is to define (or describe) its topic precisely but relatively succinctly. Describing (defining) the topic in a few paragraphs, one or two pages at most, is a part of virtually every essay and research report, although in the descriptive essay, it is the sole aim. Because descriptive essays tend to be shorter than expository or argumentative essays, purely descriptive essays are not usually required as term papers in psychology. Articles in encyclopedias illustrate brief descriptive essays—for example, a concise description of the nature of behaviorist views on language learning. In areas of clinical psychology, you will find combinations of descriptive and expository forms in case study reports (which are also considered descriptive research reports).

Incidentally, creative ability is valued in psychology courses just as it is in English courses. But when explaining or describing in psychology courses, you want to be accurate and avoid flights of fancy. An effective essay in psychology courses is not vague; it incorporates specific examples and exact quotations to support ideas.

Three Types of Research Reports

Researchers make fine distinctions between the various kinds of research approaches, such as the laboratory experiment, the sample survey, the intensive case study, and the archival approach. The study reported by Jane Doe in Appendix B illustrates another approach, an experiment in a field setting. Over and above these fine differences is another distinction among three broad types of research: the descriptive, the relational, and the experimental. Each of these has its own objective, reflected in the research report, although the report may also contain a flavor of more than one type.

First, the purpose of the *descriptive research report* is to map out its topic empirically. As an example, a student in educational psychology might write a report of how she used ethnographic methods to map out the behavior of failing pupils in a particular school. The report will describe how she observed and recorded the classroom behavior of children who were doing poorly. Her careful mapping out of the behavior of failing pupils might lead to theoretical ideas about how to revise our concepts of classroom failure and of factors that may contribute to the development of failure. These ideas could then point to testable hypotheses for relational and experimental research concerning the remediation of failure.

The careful mapping out of behavior is usually a necessary first step in the development of a program of research. Sooner or later, however, someone will want to know *how* what happens behaviorally is related to other variables. The how is the topic of the *relational research report*, which examines how events are related or how behavior is correlated with another variable. An example might be a report of a field study of the relation between children's failure in school and (a) whether the children were learning and (b) the degree to which the teacher had been exposing the children to the material to be learned. The report would examine the relationship between (b) and (a)— that is, the amount of the children's exposure to the material to be learned and the amount of such material that the children learned.

Thus, we can say that descriptive reports tell *how things are*, whereas relational reports tell *how things are in relation to other things*. The purpose of the third type, the *experimental research report*, is to tell *how things get to be the way they are*. In Appendix B, Jane Doe's report of a field experiment on the effect on tipping behavior of being offered an after-meal candy illustrates this objective. A behaviorist's example of a single-case (or N-of-1) experiment would be a report of how a child's temper outbursts at being put to bed were extinguished when proper behavioral techniques were followed.

Scheduling Time

Once you have a clear sense of your objective, the next step is to set some deadlines so you do not end up like Joe Gould, who was so paralyzed by inertia that he accomplished nothing. You know your own energy level and thought patterns, so play to your strengths. Are you a morning person? If so, block out some time to work on your writing early in the day. Do you function better at night? Then use the late hours of quiet to your advantage. Allow extra time for other pursuits by setting realistic dates by which you can reasonably expect to complete each major part of your assignment. Write the dates on your calendar; some students prefer to post the dates over their desks as daily reminders.

In planning your schedule, give yourself ample time to do a good job. Patience will pay off by making you feel more confident as you complete each task and move on to the next one. How do you know what tasks to schedule? Writing an essay usually requires spending a lot of time in the library accumulating source materials, so you will need to leave ample time for that task. Here are some ideas about what to schedule on your calendar:

Completion of literature search
Completion of proposal for essay
Completion of library work
Completion of first draft of essay
Completion of revised draft(s) of essay
Completion of final draft of essay

If you are writing a research report, you need to set aside time for the ethics review, the implementation of the research, and the data analysis. Here are some scheduling suggestions for these and other tasks:

Completion of literature search
Completion of proposal for research
Completion of ethics review
Implementation of data collection
Completion of data collection
Completion of data analysis
Completion of first draft of research report
Completion of revised draft(s) of research report
Completion of final draft of research report

Note that both schedules of tasks allow time between the first and final drafts so that you can distance yourself from your writing. Organizing, writing, and revising will take time. Library research does not always go smoothly; a book or a journal article you need might be unavailable. Data collection and analysis can also run into snags. Other problems might be that the ethics review takes longer than you expected, or you are asked to resubmit your proposal, or research subjects do not cooperate, or a computer you need is down, or research material you need is hard to find. These schedules allow you time to cope with unforeseen problems like these and time to return to your writing assignment with a fresh perspective as you polish the first draft and check for errors in logic, flow, spelling, punctuation, and grammar. By scheduling your time in this way, you should not feel pressured by imaginary deadlines—or surprised as the real deadline approaches.

If you get started early, you will also have time to track down hard-to-find reports or to locate a test you need. If you want to use a specific instrument protected by copyright, you will need to give yourself time to get permission from the publisher to use the test. Although instruments that require advanced training to administer or interpret are usually unavailable to undergraduates, a great many others are available to students. There are, in fact, general reference books that contain sample measures, such as J. P. Robinson, P. Shaver, and L. S. Wrightman's *Measures of Personality and Social Psychological Attitudes* (Academic Press, 1991), which also contains useful information about the reliability and validity of each measure.

For a comprehensive catalog of available tests and measures that you can find in journal articles and reports, you might look at the six-volume *Directory of Unpublished Experimental Mental Measures*, published by the American Psychological Association from 1995 to 1996. The "unpublished" in the title means that the instrument is generally available without a fee or special credentials. For example, Volume 6, compiled by B. A. Goldman and D. F. Mitchell, lists nearly 1,700 psychological instruments that are available for use in a wide variety of research situations, including measures of educational, psychological, social, and vocational adjustment and measures of aptitude, attitude, concept meaning, creativity, personality, problem solving, status, and so on. Exhibit 2 shows the records of six measures from this volume, and enough information is given to help you track down any particular instrument.

Starting early may also give you time to tackle data analysis procedures that are not in the course textbook. There will also be time to e-mail a researcher and request any follow-up articles that are still unpublished, if you think you need them. (Many students are surprised to learn that they can actually communicate with busy researchers and request the author's most recent work.) Another word of advice: Instructors have heard all the excuses for a late or badly done paper, so do not expect much sympathy if you miss the final deadline. If you expect to ask the instructor for a letter of recommendation for graduate school or a job, you certainly do not want to create an impression of yourself as unreliable.

Choosing a Topic

The next step is to choose a suitable topic. The selection of a topic is an integral part of learning, because usually you are free to explore experiences, observations, and ideas to help you focus on specific questions or issues that will sustain your curiosity and interest as you work on your project. If you have the time, training, and temperament to play scientific detective, you will find prematurely abandoned ideas in published research articles, such as when the researchers used test statistics that lacked sufficient power to detect an obtained effect at the desired p level. The new *Publication Manual of the American Psychological Association* is very clear on this point: "Take seriously the statistical power considerations associated with your tests of hypotheses" (p. 24). Because this was not always the case in psychological science, you can unearth missed effects and prematurely discarded hypotheses if you search the journal literature carefully.

EXHIBIT 2 Synopses of experimental mental measures

3678
Test Name: JOB CAREER KEY

Purpose: To provide a test of information about a wide variety of occupations.

Number of Items: 157

Format: A multiple-choice format is used

Reliability: Kuder-Richardson formulas ranged from .43 to .91. Test–retest (4 months) reliability (N = 19) was .62.

Author: Yanico, B. J., and Hardin, S. I.

Article: College students' self-estimated and actual knowledge of gender traditional and nontraditional occupation: A replication and extension.

Journal: *Journal of Vocational Behavior*, June 1986, *28*(3), 229–240.

Related Research: Blank, J. R. (1978). Job-career key: A test of occupational information. *Vocational Guidance Quarterly, 27*, 6–17.

3723
Test Name: MEIER BURNOUT ASSESSMENT

Purpose: To measure college student burnout.

Number of Items: 27

Format Employs a true-false format.

Reliability: Cronbach's alpha was .83.

Validity: Correlations with other variables ranged from -.13 to .62 (N = 360).

Author: McCarthy, M. E., et al.

Article: Psychological sense of community and student burnout.

Journal: *Journal of College Student Development*, May 1990, *31*(3), 211–216

Related Research: Meier, S. T., & Schmeck, R. R. (1985). The burned-out college student: A descriptive profile. *Journal of College Student Personnel, 25*, 63–69.

3705
Test Name: COMPUTER ANXIETY SCALE

Purpose: To measure the perception held by students of their anxiety in different situations related to computers.

Number of Items: 20

Format: Each item is rated on a 5-point scale ranging from *not at all* to *very much*. All items are presented.

Reliability: Test-retest (10 weeks) reliability was .77. Coefficient alpha was .97.

Author: Marcoulides, G. A.

Article: Measuring computer anxiety: The Computer Anxiety Scale.

Journal: *Educational and Psychological Measurement*, Autumn 1989, *49*(3), 733–739.

Related Research: Endler, N., & Hunt, J. (1966). Sources of behavioral variance as measured by the S-R Inventory of Anxiousness. *Psychological Bulletin, 65*, 336–339.

3993
Test Name: DATING ANXIETY SURVEY

Purpose: To assess dating anxiety in males and females.

Number of Items: 23

Format: Responses are made on a 7-point Likert scale, 1 (*being least anxious*) to 7 (*being extreme anxiety*). Includes three subscales: passive, active, and dating.

Reliability: Coefficient alphas ranged from .87 to .93 (males) and from .90 to .92 (females).

Validity: Correlations with other variables ranged from −.38 to .65.

Author: Calvert, J. D., et al.

Article: Psychometric evaluations of the Dating Anxiety Survey: A self-report questionnaire for the assessment of dating anxiety in males and females.

Journal: *Journal of Psychopathology and Behavioral Assessment*, September 1987, *9*(3), 341–350.

3710
Test Name: HASSLES SCALE

Purpose: To identify the personal severity of daily hassles as an index of student stress.

Number of items: 117

Format: Respondents indicate on a 3-point scale the severity of each relevant daily hassle. Provides two scores: frequency and intensity.

Reliability: Average test-retest reliabilities were .79 (frequency) and .48 (intensity).

Author: Elliott, T. R., and Gramling, S. E.

Article: Personal assertiveness and the effects of social support among college students.

Journal: *Journal of Counseling Psychology*, October 1990, *37*(4), 427–436.

Related Research: Kanner, A., et al. (1981). Comparison of two modes of stress measurement: Daily hassles and uplifts versus major life events. *Journal of Behavioral Medicine, 4*, 1–39.

4431
Test Name: PROCRASTINATION INVENTORY

Purpose: To measure procrastination in work-study, household chores, and interpersonal responsibilities.

Number of Items: 54

Format: Five-point self-rating scales. Sample items presented.

Reliability: Alpha was .91.

Validity: Correlations with other variables ranged from .41 (self-control) to .62 (effective study time).

Author: Stoham-Salomon, V., et al.

Article: You're changed if you do and changed if you don't: Mechanisms underlying paradoxical interventions.

Journal: *Journal of Consulting and Clinical Psychology*, October, 1989, *57*(5), 590–598.

Related Research: Sroloff, B. (1963). *An empirical research of procrastination as a state/trait phenomenon*. Unpublished Master's Thesis, Tel-Aviv University, Israel.

Ideas may also be thrust on you in unexpected ways—called *serendipity*, which implies a lucky inspiration or a fortunate coincidence. The word comes from a fairy tale about "The Three Princes of Serendip" (an ancient name for Ceylon, now known as Sri Lanka), who were constantly making lucky discoveries. A famous case of serendipity in science occurred in James Watson and Francis Crick's race (with Linus Pauling) to discover the structure of the DNA molecule and win the Nobel Prize. Watson made cardboard models, which he showed to a colleague, Jerry Donohue, a crystallographer who shared an office with Crick. Donohue's response was that the models contained mistakes, and Watson went home feeling discouraged. The next day, he was back in his office tinkering with another model when Donohue happened to walk in. Watson asked Donohue whether he had any objections to the new model, and when he answered no, Watson's morale soared, as he realized that he might now have the answer to the DNA riddle. In his book *The Double Helix* (Atheneum, 1968), Watson wrote that, had it not been for the lucky dividend of Donohue's sharing an office with Crick, Crick and Watson would not have won this race for the Nobel prize.

In considering a suitable topic, beware of a few pitfalls; the following are dos and don'ts that might make your life easier as you start choosing a topic:

- ◆ Do use the indexes and tables of contents of standard textbooks as well as your class notes for initial leads or ideas to explore more fully.
- ◆ Do choose a topic that piques your curiosity.
- ◆ Do make sure your topic can be covered in the available time and in the assigned number of pages.
- ◆ Don't be afraid to ask your instructor for suggestions.
- ◆ Don't choose a topic that you know other students have chosen; you will be competing with them for access to the library's source material.

Narrowing the Topic

Choosing too broad or too narrow a topic will add difficulties and mean an unsatisfactory result. A proposed essay that is too broad—for example, "Sigmund Freud's Life and Times"—would try to cover too much material within the limited framework of the assignment and the time available to complete it. A specific aspect of Freud's theoretical work would prove a more appropriately narrowed focus for treatment in an essay for a course on personality theories, abnormal behavior, or psychopathology.

In narrowing the essay topic, do not limit your discussion just to facts that are already well known. There are two simple guidelines:

- ◆ Be sure that your topic is not so narrow that reference materials will be hard to find.
- ◆ Be guided by your instructor's advice because the instructor can help you avoid taking on an unwieldy topic.

If you approach instructors with several concrete ideas, you will usually find them glad to help tailor those ideas so that you, the topic, and the project format are compatible. Here are examples of how you might shape the working title of a proposed essay for a one-semester course:

Unlimited Topic (Much Too Broad)
"Psychological Theories of Sigmund Freud"

Slightly Limited Topic
"Freud's Theory of Dreams"

Limited to 20-Page Paper
"Freud's Theory of Oedipal Conflict Applied to Mental Health"

Limited to 10-Page Paper
"Freud's Theory of Infantile Sexuality"

You can always polish the title later, once you have finished your literature search, have read what you found, and have a better sense of the topic. Here is another example of shaping a topic for a one-semester course. This time the assignment is for an empirical research project:

Unlimited Topic (Too Broad for a Term Project)
"How Do People Differ in Their Ability to Decipher Nonverbal Messages?"

Slightly Limited Topic
"How Do Men and Women Differ in Their Ability to Decipher Nonverbal Messages?"

Adequately Limited Topic
"How Do Male and Female Intro Psych Students at Podunk U. Differ in Their Ability to Decipher Joy, Disappointment, Anger, and Fear in Photographed Facial Expressions of Women and Men?"

If you are currently enrolled in a research methods course, your text probably discusses criteria for assessing the merits of hypotheses. A detailed discussion is beyond the scope of this manual, but we can mention three criteria:

◆ Hypotheses for scientific research should be grounded in credible ideas and facts. In other words, you must do a literature search to find out whether your hypotheses are consistent with accepted findings in the scientific literature. If they are not, then you will need to think about the inconsistencies and decide (with the help of the instructor) whether you really have a fresh insight or will need to develop some other hypotheses.

◆ State your hypotheses in a precise and focused way. To ensure that you are using technical terms correctly, you can consult resources in the library (encyclopedias of psychology, for example). To ensure that your hypotheses are focused, you can consult your instructor, who will show you how to cut away unwieldy words and ideas.

◆ Hypotheses and predictions must be falsifiable if they are incorrect. Hypotheses that are not refutable by any conceivable empirical means are considered unscientific. For example, the statement "All behavior is a product of the good and evil lying within us" does not qualify as a valid scientific hypothesis: It is so vague and amorphous that it cannot be subjected to empirical refutation.

Knowing Your Audience and Topic

All professional writers know that they are writing for a particular audience. This knowledge helps them determine the tone and style of their work. Think of a journalist's report of a house fire and contrast it with a short story describing the same event. Knowing one's audience is no less important when the writer is a college student and the project is an essay or a research report. The main audience is your instructor. Should you have any questions about the instructor's grading criteria, find out what they are before you start to work.

For example, in a course on research methods, one instructor's syllabus contained the following grading criteria for different parts of the finished report (the numbers in parentheses are percentages):

Abstract
    Informativeness (5)
Introduction
    Clarity of purpose (10)
    Literature review (10)
Method
    Adequacy of design (10)
    Quality and completeness of description (10)
Results
    Appropriateness and correctness of analysis (10)
    Use of tables or figures (5)
    Clarity of presentation (10)
Discussion
    Interpretation of results (10)
    Critique/future directions (10)
Miscellaneous
    Organization, style, references, etc. (5)
    Appendix for raw data and calculations (5)

This kind of information enabled the students to concentrate on different parts of the assignment in the same way that the instructor would concentrate on them when evaluating the reports. This information can also serve as a checklist for you to make sure that everything of importance is covered adequately in your finished report. Not every instructor will provide such detailed information about grading, but this manual can help you compose your own checklist based on other information the instructor has provided.

Cultivating an Understanding

Let us assume that you know what your main audience—your instructor—expects of you. Now you must try to develop more than a superficial understanding of your topic. The more you read about it and discuss your ideas with friends, the more you will begin to cultivate an intuitive understanding of the topic. In the next chapter, we describe how to use library and computerized resources to nurture this understanding. Here are two tips to get you started:

- ◆ Some writers find it helpful to keep several 3 × 5-inch cards handy, or to use sticky notes, for jotting down relevant ideas that suddenly occur to them. This is a good way to keep your topic squarely in your mind.
- ◆ You must also comprehend your source material, so equip yourself with a good desk dictionary, and turn to it routinely whenever you come across an unfamiliar word. It is a habit that will serve you well.

The most comprehensive dictionaries are labeled *unabridged* (which means that they have not been shortened in size by the omission of terms or definitions), and the most comprehensive of all dictionaries in the English language is the multivolume *Oxford English Dictionary* (called for short the *OED*). It gives the origin and history of words in the English language from the year A.D. 1150 to the publication of the *OED*. To illustrate, suppose you were going to study gossip and began by looking the term up in the *OED*. You would find that the word *gossip* began quite innocently as *god-sibbs*, for "godparents," meaning those with spiritual affinity to the child being baptized. Christenings were occasions for distant relatives to be present and an opportunity to share news. In the same way that the *d* in *God's spell* was dropped to form *gospel*, *god-sibbs* led to *gossip*. Although gossip has acquired a distinctly pejorative and feminine connotation, were you to continue your search by using a computer to retrieve abstracts of the published studies of gossip, you would learn that these investigations have implicated several different functions of gossip as well as shown that men also engage in it (but often call it something else, such as *shop talk* or *shooting the breeze*).

In the next chapter we will discuss how to do an on-line search of databases that can point you to articles and books that are relevant to your own topic of interest. Some databases contain the complete text of certain reference works and journals, and your college library may have an arrangement whereby you can access the full-text resources in your room (peruse the *OED*, for example); all this is discussed in the next chapter. Incidentally, a recent book that is bound to whet your interest in the *OED* is *The Professor and the Madman: A Tale of Murder, Insanity, and the Making of the Oxford University Dictionary* (Harper, 1998) by Simon Winchester.

2

FINDING AND USING
REFERENCE MATERIALS

The literature review is an essential step in writing a research report
or an essay because it puts your own ideas in context, building on
existing work by others. Knowing about the many search tools
available will allow you to gauge the effort it will take to do a
review. If you know how to retrieve the information you need
electronically, you can save time and effort. This chapter shows
you how to use electronic and print resources most effectively to
gather background information.

Using the Library

Let us assume you have an idea for an essay or a research project, have spoken about it in a very preliminary way with your instructor, and know that you must produce a written proposal. In the next chapter we will discuss the nature of the proposal for an essay topic or a research study. However, before you begin drafting your proposal, you will need to identify and examine relevant work on the topic in which you are interested. You will use a computer to do a PsycINFO search of the literature, and then you will need to find and read the articles and books summarized in the abstracts that you retrieved. If the full-text version of those materials is not available online, you will look in the library for the original sources. Later on, if you decide to do a further search of other electronic databases, you will probably need to spend additional time in the library to gather the materials you need to flesh out your final paper. So if you have never set foot in the library, now is the time to get oriented.

College libraries generally have a specialized area (traditionally called the *information desk*) where patrons can ask for information. But it may not be convenient to return to this area every time you have a question, so you can see if there is a fact sheet (and floor plan) describing other areas where you can ask staff members (often called *information specialists*) for assistance. Find out where photocopiers are located and whether you need to bring coins or purchase a card in order to use them. It is a lot easier to photocopy a page from a journal or book than to copy lengthy passages by hand, and having a photocopy will ensure that you have the information as it appears in the original source. If you have your own computer, you might ask how you can access the library's electronic databases, including any that require a special connection to read and download.

There is also usually a reference desk, where staff members who are true generalists are available to answer all manner of questions or at least point you to sources to help you answer them yourself. They may suggest reference works (an encyclopedia or a serial publication, for example) that are "not circulated" (cannot be checked out) but can be used in a specified section of the library. Suppose you wanted to find information about a particular psychological test; they might point you to the *Mental Measurements Yearbook* for such information as the population for intended use, forms, cost, author(s), publisher, cross-references to previous editions, and references to authoritative reviews, journal articles, books, and dissertations that discuss the test. If you want a book or a journal that is unavailable in your college library, you can ask at the reference desk about an *interlibrary loan*.

Other specialized areas are the circulation desk, the reserve area, and the current periodicals area. The circulation desk is where you check out books and any other materials, return these materials, and take care of overdue notices. Bring a photo ID with you. The reserve area is for books, photocopies of journal articles, and other material that instructors have placed "on hold" or "on reserve" (not to be circulated). You can examine this material only in the library and for a specified period (2 hours, for example). The current periodicals area is where you find recent issues of journals, magazines, and newspapers. Some periodicals can be viewed online in full-text databases linked to the library's Web site; this process not only conserves space but also prevents the problem of missing or damaged copies and expands the storehouse of available information as libraries share their resources through interconnected computers. (For definitions of common terms and jargon used on the Web, see Exhibit 3.)

However, suppose all you want now is to find a particular book in the stacks. You will need the *call number*, because the stacks are coded according to certain categories that coincide with call numbers. To find out how the book has been classified, you will use a computer to look up the book's call number in the library's automated catalog. For identification, the call number is also printed on the bottom of the book's spine. Exhibit 4 shows the two systems of classification most frequently used in U.S. libraries: the Library of Congress System and the Dewey Decimal System. For psychology students, these two systems may be puzzling, however, because psychological material is classified under several different headings. The Library of Congress System divides material into 20 major groups, and abnormal psychology books, for

EXHIBIT 3 Common terms and jargon on the Web

attachment: a digitally coded file that is downloaded when you specifically open an add-on to an e-mail message; the attachment might contain words, images, or, in a worst case scenario, a hidden virus.

browser: a program (such as Internet Explorer or Netscape) that is used to display Web pages.

cache: a place on the computer's hard drive where images and text from visited Web pages are stored to speed up the process of downloading the next time they are visited. Caches can, however, clutter the hard drive, particularly when information on the Web pages is constantly updated, so it is a good idea to clean the cache occasionally.

cookies: bits of personalized information left on the hard drive by some Web sites so they can track visitors online. There are cookie cleanup programs (we use Norton Systemworks) to send this information into oblivion, but some Web sites will not admit visitors unless they agree to accept a cookie.

database: a collection of data, such as the reference databases shown in Exhibit 9.

firewall: a system that protects online computers from outside hackers who want to steal information or create a launching pad for destructive signals to Web sites.

full-text database: textual material that can be electronically perused in its entirety, such as the complete content of a journal article, a book, a dictionary, or an encyclopedia.

html: the coded language (Hypertext Markup Language) used to create Web pages.

http: acronym for Hypertext Transfer Protocol, the prefix (http://) of many URLs; it signifies the way that computers communicate with one another on the Internet.

hyperlink: a coded image (an icon or a button) or a coded word or phrase (usually in blue and underlined) that changes to a hand when you move your mouse pointer over it; clicking the hyperlink transports you to another place.

Internet service provider: the company or organization providing access to the Internet, such as AOL (America Online) and MSN (Microsoft Network), or a telephone or cable company.

JPEG: acronym for Joint Photographic Experts Group, which is the most popular format on the Internet for photos because it supports 24-bit color and subtle variations in brightness and hue.

online search: using a computer and a search engine to retrieve information.

search engine: a program that takes key words, queries an internal index, and returns a set of Web documents. Our favorite search engine is Google (http://www.google.com); other popular ones are HotBot, AltaVista, Lycos, InfoSeek, Excite, and Metacrawler.

spam: unsolicited e-mail that is automatically sent to all those on an address list.

URL: acronym for Uniform Resource Locator, which is another name for the Web address. The URL of a helpful Web site created at the University of Waterloo, which contains links to national and international psychological societies (including the American Psychological Association and the American Psychological Society, which post information about student funding and career planning), is http://www.lib.uwaterloo.ca/society/psychol_soc.html. If you are interested in the field of social psychology, you might check the Social Psychology Network at http://www.socialpsychology.org, created at Wesleyan University by Dr. Scott Plous.

viruses: damaging codes that invade a computer's hard drive when an infected attachment or a contaminated file is opened. Some viruses, called *worms*, copy themselves and spread rapidly in the hard drive; others, called *Trojan horses*, assume the appearance of normal files but secretly wipe the hard drive clean. As a safeguard against viruses, be cautious about what you download or open, and install (and routinely update, usually weekly) antivirus software (such as Norton Anti-Virus) to check attachments before you open them and, in a worst case scenario, to find and try to repair damage to your hard drive.

EXHIBIT 4   Two systems of classification used in U.S. libraries

Library of Congress System		Dewey Decimal System	
A	General works	000	General works
B	Philosophy and religion	100	Philosophy
C	General history	200	Religion
D	Foreign history	300	Social sciences
E-F	America	400	Language
G	Geography and anthropology	500	Natural sciences
H	Social sciences	600	Technology
J	Political science	700	Fine arts
K	Law	800	Literature
L	Education	900	History and geography
M	Music		
N	Fine arts		
P	Language and literature		
Q	Science		
R	Medicine		
S	Agriculture		
T	Technology		
U	Military science		
V	Naval science		
Z	Bibliography and library science		

example, can be found under BF or RC. The Dewey Decimal System classifies material under 10 headings (and abnormal psychology can be found in the 157 class).

Some libraries attempt to protect their collection of books by restricting access to the stacks. If you find yourself unable to access the stacks directly, you submit a form that lists the call number of the book you want to use and a staff member then retrieves it for you. If you are allowed to browse in the stacks, refer to Exhibit 5. It shows the cataloging of more specific areas by both systems. Browsing can lead you to a valuable but unexpected book or to a pertinent quote that illustrates some idea or point. But do not get side-tracked by irrelevant material; keep focused on the purpose of your search.

To help you get further oriented, we will look over the shoulder of a student named Eric as he goes step by step through the process of doing a literature search. At this stage, all that he is interested in is gathering sufficient background information to formulate a testable hypothesis and then write an acceptable proposal. First, we describe the big picture; then, we examine the details of the resources used by Eric. Afterward, we describe other resources that are usually available to students in college libraries or electronically through their Web sites.

EXHIBIT 5 *Cataloging of psychological materials in U.S. libraries*

Library of Congress System		*Dewey Decimal System*	
BF	Abnormal psychology	00-	Artificial intelligence
	Child psychology	13-	Parapsychology
	Cognition	15-	Abnormal psychology
	Comparative psychology		Child psychology
	Environmental psychology		Cognitive psychology
	Motivation		Comparative psychology
	Parapsychology		Environmental psychology
	Perception		Industrial psychology
	Personality		Motivation
	Physiological psychology		Perception
	Psycholinguistics		Personality
	Psychological statistics		Physiological psychology
HF	Industrial psychology	30-	Family
	Personnel management		Psychology of women
HM	Social psychology		Social psychology
HQ	Family	37-	Educational psychology
	Psychology of women		Special education
LB	Educational psychology	40-	Psycholinguistics
LC	Special education	51-	Statistics
Q	Artificial intelligence	61-	Psychiatry
	Physiological psychology		Psychotherapy
QA	Mathematical statistics	65-	Personnel management
RC	Abnormal psychology		
	Psychiatry		
	Psychotherapy		
T	Personnel management		

Looking Over Eric's Shoulder

Eric thinks he wants to study a spin-off from the instructor's lecture on what she called the "Pygmalion experiment," a classic research study by Robert Rosenthal and Lenore Jacobson. In a book the instructor mentioned, called *Pygmalion in the Classroom*, Rosenthal and Jacobson described how, in the spring of 1964, they had given a standard nonverbal intelligence test to all the children in a public elementary school in South San Francisco. The teachers were told only that the test was one of intellectual "blooming," and approximately 20% of the children (whose names the investigators had simply picked at random) were represented to the teachers as capable of marked intellectual growth based on the children's performance on this test. In other words, the difference between the supposed potential bloomers and the other students existed solely in the minds of their teachers. The children's performance on the intelligence test was measured after one semester, again after a full academic year, and again after two academic years. The results of this experiment revealed that, although the greatest differential gain in total intelligence appeared after one school year, the bloomers held an advantage over the other children even after two years. Eric's instructor described these results as an example of what are more generally called *expectancy effects* in social psychology.

Eric mentions his interest in the Pygmalion experiment to the instructor, and she suggests he read Rosenthal and Jacobson's book and look up an article by Stephen Raudenbush, published in the 1980s, in which he reported the results of a meta-analysis (i.e., a quantitative synthesis) he performed of all the Pygmalion experiments up to that time. She is not sure where the article was published but thinks it might have been in the *Journal of Educational Psychology*. She suggests that Eric do an author search using PsycINFO to find this article. She also recommends he look up *expectancy effect* and *Pygmalion experiment* in any recent encyclopedias of psychology that the library has, and that he use PsycINFO to do a more extensive retrieval of abstracts after he has identified the key synonyms. While he is on the library's Web page, he can see if there is a list of other electronic databases that might be useful later on, she adds.

Eric begins by using the library's online catalog to find the call number of Rosenthal and Jacobson's book: LB1131.R585. It means that, to find this book, he must go to the LB section of the stacks and, next, to the more specific section in numerical (1131) and then alphanumerical order (R585). If this book is not in the stacks, he can ask at the reference desk for help in locating it or, if the material is lost, for help in borrowing a copy through an interlibrary loan. Fortunately, he finds the book and takes it to the circulation desk to check it out. While there, he asks about encyclopedias of psychology, and the librarian points him to the location of several recent ones. He looks up the key term *expectancy effect* in the indexes, reads the material, and finds that expectancy effects are also referred to as *experimenter expectancy effects*, and sometimes as *Rosenthal effects*, because Robert Rosenthal did so much landmark research on the topic. He takes notes, including making a list of relevant references and recommended readings cited in the encyclopedias, which he will look into later.

To find the article by Stephen Raudenbush, Eric uses the computer to access the library's online reference databases. In the list on the library's Web site, he finds PsycINFO and clicks on it. He then simply checks "Author" and types "Raudenbush" and clicks on the SEARCHES button, which gives him a long list of published works by this author. Each item on the list links with a PsycINFO record that also provides an abstract of the work. He scrolls down the list until he recognizes the article that his teacher mentioned and prints out the PsycINFO record (see Exhibit 6), planning to find the article later in

EXHIBIT 6 PsycINFO *record of journal articles*

Record 1 of 1 in PsycINFO 1984-1987

AN: 1984-16218-001

DT: Journal-Article

TI: Magnitude of teacher expectancy effects on pupil IQ as a function of the credibility of expectancy induction: A synthesis of findings from 18 experiments.

AU: **Raudenbush,-Stephen-W**

SO: Journal-of-Educational-Psychology. 1984 Feb; Vol 76(1): 85-97

PB: US: American Psychological Assn.

IS: 0022-0663

PY: 1984

AB: Meta-analysis was used to examine the variability in the outcomes of experiments testing the effects of teacher expectancy on pupil IQ. The tenuous process of expectancy induction, wherein researchers supply teachers with information designed to elevate their expectancies for children actually selected at random, is viewed as problematic in "Pygmalion" experiments, as developed by R. Rosenthal and L. Jacobson (1968). It was hypothesized that the better teachers know their pupils at the time of expectancy induction, the smaller the treatment effect would be. Data strongly support this hypothesis. Hypotheses that the type of IQ test (groups vs. individual) and type of test administrator (aware vs blind to expectancy-inducing information) influence experimental results were not supported. The hypothesis that expectancy effects are larger for children in Grades 1 and 2 than for children in Grades 3-6 was supported. However, significant effects reappeared at Grade 7. Theoretical implications and questions for future meta-analytic research are discussed. (57 ref) (PsycINFO Database Record (c) 2000 APA, all rights reserved)(unassigned)

---

the library and photocopy relevant parts. Articles published recently in APA (American Psychological Association) and some other journals are available electronically through the PsycARTICLES database, which is linked with PsycINFO, but Eric will have to track down this one in the library.

Having done all this, Eric has mastered about all the skills it will take to use any other of the library's electronic databases to do a detailed search. He has learned that reference databases allow you to customize the information that comes up on the screen. Each icon (or button) does something useful, and there is a HELP button if you are not sure. On the PsycINFO site, Eric checks off the years to which he wants to limit his search of the literature. All he is interested in is drumming up a good hypothesis, so he feels he needs to check only the last 3 years. Without changing any of the fields that will be returned by the search, he just enters the first thing that comes into his head: "expect*" (no quote marks). The "*" is like a wild card that tells the computer to search for any ending: "expects," "expecting," "expectancy," "expectations," and so on. Eric gets 6,901 returns, far too many. He tries "expecta*" and gets 3,877, still too many. He tries "expectancy" and gets 639—better. "Expectancy effects" gives him 22 returns—maybe too few, but maybe not. To find out for sure, he peruses the list to see what turned up.

There is a tiny box at the beginning of each record in the list that he can check for later printing or saving, or he can save the whole file without checking anything. Because he brought a blank disk with him, he saves the file on his disk. Saving the file can be a great time saver if the library printing station is very busy. Later, he can edit the list and print it at his leisure (freeing up the library computer sooner, too). Eric notices how he can choose which fields show in each record, although he usually just selects "ALL" of them. He always includes the search history, thinking that he may need to replicate the search or may want to describe it in the method section of his research report to show how he discovered his sources.

Reference databases have their own "limited vocabularies," sets of words and phrases (called *descriptors*) regarding a topic. PsycINFO refers to its set as a "Thesaurus." Eric clicks on this button and discovers a few more phrases to search with: "teacher expectations" returns 34; "teacher student interaction," 499; and a combination of these two, 2. He checks out the 2 records and then redisplays the list of 34 to save on his disk and peruse later. He tries a few more searches just for fun—and because they take only seconds to execute.

The SEARCHES button displays the history of Eric's search efforts, allowing easy review and also a combining of search sets. By saving the search history in his output, he can use the same search pattern again if his project requires a more extensive search later on. However, his search has turned up more than enough material for him to write his proposal. He is astonished, in fact, to see he has done 11 searches in a very short time. He happens to notice that he misspelled a word in one of his searches; when he corrects the spelling, he gets three records instead of none. He wonders at the amazing flexibility and speed of the search engine. Just about anything he might want to do with the returned records he *can* do. He can sort the output by any field at all. For example, he can research a particular author by sorting on the author's last name. Ask yourself what would be convenient for your purposes, and chances are the programmers have also thought of it and incorporated it.

So far, Eric has invested only a few hours at the library doing these searches, scanning and saving the relevant titles and abstracts to see if they might help him. The next step will be to read the abstracts, cull the list for those that seem most relevant, track the full works in the library or electronically in a full-text database, read, and take notes. Afterward, Eric will consult again with his instructor before settling on a research design and beginning work on his proposal (discussed in Chapter Three).

EXHIBIT 7   Library of Congress online record of book

```
LC Control Number:     68019667
Type of Material:      Book (Print, Microform, Electronic, etc.)
Personal Name:         Rosenthal, Robert, 1933-
Main Title:            Pygmalion in the classroom; teacher expectation
                       and pupils' intellectual development [by] Robert
                       Rosenthal [and] Lenore Jacobson.
Published/Created:     New York, Holt, Rinehart and Winston [1968]
Related Names:         Jacobson, Lenore, joint author.
Description:           xi, 240 p. illus. 23 cm.
ISBN:                  0030688051
                       0030686857 (college ed.)
Notes:                 Bibliography: p. 219-229.
Subjects:              Prediction of scholastic success.
                       Children--Intelligence levels.
LC Classification:     LB1131 .R585
Dewey Class No.:       372.12/64 19
                       ---------------------
CALL NUMBER:           LB1131 .R585
                       Copy 1
-- Request in:         Jefferson or Adams Bldg General or Area Studies
                       Reading Rms
-- Status:             Not Charged
```

Using the Automated Card Catalog

Eric began his work by using the automated card catalog (called for short the *automated catalog* or *online catalog*) to find the location of Rosenthal and Jacobson's *Pygmalion in the Classroom* in the library's stacks. Libraries in the United States do not all use the same online program, but all provide the same basic information to patrons. If you go to the Web site of the Library of Congress Online Catalog in Washington, DC (www.lcWeb.loc.gov/catalog), and look up the Rosenthal and Jacobson book, you will find the record that is reprinted in Exhibit 7. If your library still has a card catalog that you can use (usually near the reference desk), the information in Exhibit 7 is similar to what you will see in the card catalog. The name *card catalog*, incidentally, comes from the miles and miles of three types of alphabetized 3 × 5-inch cards cataloged in file drawers: (a) author cards, (b) title cards, and (c) subject cards. If the card catalog no longer exists in your college library, it is because it has been completely replaced by an automated (online) catalog.

Assuming your library has a card catalog, you might look up Rosenthal and Jacobson's book. Exhibit 8 shows the card you will find under "Rosenthal, Robert" or "Jacobson, Lenore" (author card) or "Pygmalion in the classroom" (title card). Notice the similarity of information to that in the online record in Exhibit 7. For most students, the most significant information is

EXHIBIT 8 *Catalog card for book in Exhibit 7*

LB
1131
R585

Rosenthal, Robert, 1933—
    Pygmalion in the classroom; teacher expectation and pupils'
intellectual development [by] Robert Rosenthal [and] Lenore
Jacobson. New York, Holt, Rinehart and Winston [1968]
    xi, 240 p. illus. 23 cm
    Bibliography: p. 219–229.

    1. Prediction of scholastic success. 2. Mental tests. I.
Jacobson, Lenore, joint author. II. Title.

LB1131.R585   372.1'2'644   68–19667

Library of Congress

---

simply the call number, which you see on the upper left of the catalog card
(Exhibit 8) and toward the bottom of the online record (Exhibit 7). The online record mentions something called the *ISBN numbers* (standing for International Standard Book Number), which are code numbers, assigned by the
publisher, that identifies this book. Both the catalog card and the online
record show the name and birth date of the first author (Rosenthal, Robert,
1933–). Beneath are the title of the book and its subtitle ("teacher expectation
and pupils' intellectual development"), followed by the complete list of authors in the order in which they appear on the title page of the book. Then
follows the location and name of the publisher (New York, Holt, Rinehart
and Winston) and the date of copyright (1968). One additional piece of useful information on the electronic record are buildings or places where copies
of the book can be found. The remainder of the information consists of technical details for librarians.

    If you are interested, the information in the middle of the card (Exhibit 8)
shows the number of prefatory pages (xi) and the length of the book (240 p.);
it also indicates that the book contains figures or other illustrations (illus.),
that it stands 23 cm high on the shelf, and that the bibliography or list of references is on pages 219–229. The section below indicates the categories under
which this book should be cataloged ("Mental tests," for example). Next is
the book's Library of Congress classification number again (LB1131.R585),
the Dewey decimal classification number of this work (372.1'2'644), the
order number of this particular set of cards (68–19667), and from whom the
cards can be ordered (Library of Congress).

EXHIBIT 9 *Sample of reference databases accessible online*

Name	Coverage
AskERIC	Bibliographic records of research reports, conference papers, teaching guides, books, and journal articles in education from preschool to the doctoral level; ERIC is an acronym for Educational Resources Information Center
booksinprint.com	Full-text reviews of books in print, as well as out-of-print listings over the last decade
britannica.com	Full-text database for *Encyclopedia Britannica* and *Merriam-Webster's Collegiate Dictionary*
Census Lookup	Produced by the U.S. Census Bureau, offers access to data tables for specific types of geographic areas from the most recent Census of Population and Housing
CQ Library	Full-text database for *CQ Weekly* and *CQ Researcher*, which provide legislative news about what is happening on Capitol Hill
EDGAR	Acronym for Electronic Data Gathering, Analysis, and Retrieval System, this is the Securities and Exchange Commission's database of electronic filings
Electronic Human Relations Area Files	Acronym is eHRAF; this nonprofit institution at Yale University is a consortium of educational, research, cultural, and government agencies in over 30 countries that provides ethnographic and related information by culture and subject
GPO Access	U.S. Government Printing Office full-text documents and other informational links
Harrison's Online	Full text of *Harrison's Principles of Internal Medicine*, a well-known medical textbook
Internet Grateful Med	Health-related search information, including links to MEDLINE (national and international references to millions of articles in medicine, biomedicine, and related fields), AIDSLINE, HIST-LINE (History of Medicine Online), and other Web sites

Using Other Electronic Databases

Eric used PsycINFO, the APA's primary abstract database. The advantage of computer-readable databases like this one, as Eric discovered, is that patrons can search to their hearts' content. College libraries usually have a bank of computers reserved for students. Because you may have to wait your turn to use one, it is a good idea to find out whether there are computers in other locations that you can use to communicate with the automated system and, if you have your own computer, how to access these resources from your room.

Exhibit 9 gives a flavor of some of the many electronic databases that are often available to students through their library's Web page. There are databases for just about every discipline and area of interest, and it is easy and fun to use them. Here are some tips:

EXHIBIT 9 *Continued*

Name	Coverage
JSTOR	Full text of periodicals in ecology, economics, education, finance, history, mathematics, political science, and population studies
LEXIS-NEXIS Academic UNIVerse	Full text of news reports, including business, medical, political, financial, and legal; a convenient source of news reports by topic areas
MathSciNet	Research literature in mathematics, with emphasis on data in *Mathematical Reviews* and *Current Mathematical Publications*
NCJRS Database	National Criminal Justice Reference Service database, including summaries of publications on criminal justice
New Grove Dictionary	Full text of *The New Grove Dictionary of Music and Musicians* and *The New Grove Dictionary of Opera*
OED Online	Full text of 20-volume *Oxford English Dictionary* and additions
ProQuest Direct	Records of scholarly journals, periodicals, newspapers, and magazines in the University of Michigan archives, including charts, maps, photos, and some literature in full-text format
PsycARTICLES	The American Psychological Association's full-text database of thousands of contemporary journal articles.
PsycINFO	The American Psychological Association's abstract database, including every abstract created by the APA back to 1887 in all areas of psychology. The print version of PsycINFO is called *Psychological Abstracts*, but there is not an exact correspondence between records on these two archival databases.
Web of Science	Access to *Social Sciences Citation Index* (*SSCI*), the parent source of titles of works and names of authors, from 1989 to the present, as well as the *Science Citation Index* (also from 1989 forward)

- ◆ Begin by writing down the questions you have, and then make a list of words or phrases you want to use as descriptors.
- ◆ Scan the list of the databases that are available to you online; print the list if you can, which is better than trying to remember them or endlessly going back and forth.
- ◆ Besides PsycINFO, put a check mark next to any others that look relevant now or that might be of interest later on.
- ◆ As you search, keep a record so that you do not backtrack without realizing it; list the abstract or index, the years searched, and the search terms that you used.
- ◆ If you can, copy what you find on a disk that you can scan again later; before you open this file (or download it to your own hard drive), use your antivirus program to ensure that the file is not infected.

◆ Do not just make a citation list of relevant work; also read what you are going to cite because the instructor will wonder whether you have read it.

Another specialized electronic resource, not listed in Exhibit 9, is one that you will find fascinating and enormously valuable if you are interested in classics in the history of psychology. This Web site (http://psychclassics.yorku.ca) was created by Dr. Christopher D. Greer at York University in Canada. Material is easy to retrieve, and you will be astounded by the vast number of original documents that are available electronically if you simply enter a famous name (Pavlov or Freud, for example) and click on your mouse.

Other Resources in the Library

Of course, you do not want to restrict yourself only to electronic resources. A great many other useful dictionaries and reference sources are also usually available in libraries. There are, for example, slang dictionaries that can tell you the history of rhyming slang, African-American slang, pig Latin, and so forth. If you are interested in information about people in the news or other prominent people, you can look in *Current Biography* or *Who's Who*. If you want to know about famous Americans from the past, you can look in the *Dictionary of American Biography* or *Who Was Who in America*. The *Dictionary of National Biography* tells about men and women in British history. Librarians can point you to other works that you may find useful. Just remember that librarians are highly skilled in helping students find material. No matter how busy the librarian looks, you should not be intimidated. Do not be afraid to approach a librarian for help in finding resource material; that is the librarian's main purpose.

Another useful library resource is the *Annual Review of Psychology*, which is a serial publication (that is, published at regular intervals). There are *Annual Reviews* for just about every subject in science, each consisting of detailed review/synthesis articles by leading authorities on specialized topics. Looking in the reference section of the *Annual Review of Psychology*, for example, can be a good way to find key studies. Other useful resources in psychology are called *handbooks*; if you search on this term in your library's automated catalog, you are likely to find several specialized handbooks. These edited books also contain detailed reviews, and although the emphasis of handbook chapters tends to be more idiosyncratic than the *Annual Review* or the articles in encyclopedias, perusing several of these resources can help you formulate an overall picture of the particular area of research in which you are interested.

Some journals also specialize in integrative reviews. One of these is the highly respected *Psychological Bulletin* (a bimonthly publication of the APA). Another excellent journal is the more recently inaugurated *Review of General Psychology* (a quarterly journal of the APA's Division of General Psychology).

Two other highly respected journals, *Psychological Review* (a quarterly APA journal) and *Behavioral and Brain Sciences* (a quarterly published by Cambridge University Press), are other excellent sources of integrative articles. One special feature of *Behavioral and Brain Sciences* is that, after each article, there is a section (called "Open Peer Commentary") where you will find lively commentary on the article by other researchers.

SSCI and the Web of Science

Among the reference databases listed in Exhibit 9 is the Web of Science, which provides online access to relatively recent records in the *Social Sciences Citation Index* (*SSCI*) and the *Science Citation Index* (*SCI*). It is not difficult to use the printed form of the *SSCI*, for example, to do an ancestry search of citations of books and journal articles in the social and behavioral sciences. The term *ancestry search* simply means tracking "ancestral" citations of an article or a book back to a specified year. Both the *SSCI* and the *SCI* list, in alphabetical order by the last name of the first author, the particular year's published literature that cited the work in question.

To illustrate, when we looked up "Robert Rosenthal" and then listed under his name the book "*Pygmalion in the Classroom*" in the year 1992 *SSCI*, we found the list of entries shown in Exhibit 10. Each entry gives the author of a work that refers to this book (for example, Ambady, N.), the source of the work (*Psychological Bulletin*), the volume number (111), the beginning page number (256), the year of publication (1992), and, in this case, a code letter (*R*) indicating that the work is a review of the literature. Other code letters used by the *SSCI* are *C* for corrections; *D* for discussions (conference items); *L* for letters; *M* for meeting abstracts; *N* for technical notes; *RP* for reprint; and *W* for computer reviews (hardware, software, and database reviews). The absence of a code letter means that the work is an article, a report, a technical paper, or the like.

The *Science Citation Index (SCI)* is a companion index to the *SSCI* and is usually next to the *SSCI* in the stacks, so it might pay you to look in both indexes if you are doing an exhaustive search for a bibliography (that is, a complete list of readings). The Web of Science, assuming it is available on your library's Web site, is as easy to use as PsycINFO but, at this time, goes back only to 1989, whereas the printed form of *SSCI* and *SCI* go as far back as 1966.

The Fugitive Literature

Work that is unpublished, or hard to find, is termed the *fugitive literature* (or *gray literature*). For example, some private institutions and government agencies fund research that may be circulated only in technical reports. Sometimes this material is available online, unless it is confidential or a privileged communication. Incidentally, dissertations and theses that graduate students write can often be found online as well. The AskERIC database is the place to look

EXHIBIT 10   SSCI citations of Pygmalion in the Classroom

68 Pygmalion Classroom

Ambady N	Psychol B	111	256	92	R
Aronson JM	J Exp S Psy	28	277	92	
Berliner DC	Educ Psych	27	143	92	
Carnelle KB	J Soc Pers	9	5	92	
Deci EL	Educ Psych	26	325	91	
Ensminge ME	Sociol Educ	65	95	92	
Epstein EH	Ox Rev Educ	18	201	92	
Feingold A	Psychol B	111	304	92	R
Gaynor JLR	J Creat Beh	26	108	92	
Goldenbe C	Am Educ Res	29	517	92	
Haring KA	T Ear Child	12	151	92	
Jussim L	J Pers Soc	62	402	92	
"	"	63	947	92	
Kershaw T	J Black St	23	152	92	
Kravetz S	Res Dev Dis	13	145	92	
Mayes LC	J Am Med A	267	406	92	
McDiarmi GW	J Teach Edu	43	83	92	
McGorry PD	Aust Nz J P	26	3	92	R
Milich R	Sch Psych R	21	400	92	
Musser LM	Bas Appl Ps	12	441	91	
Schwartz CA	Library Q	62	123	92	R
Semmel MI	J Spec Educ	25	415	92	
Spangenb ER	J Publ Pol	11	26	92	
Suen HK	T Ear Child	12	66	92	

Source: Reprinted from the *Social Sciences Citation Index,* ® Year 1992, Volume 3, with the permission of the Institute for Scientific Information® (ISI), © copyright 1992.

for selected conference papers in education, and ProQuest Digital Dissertations is where to find unpublished dissertations in the University of Michigan's archives.

You can also e-mail the author of a technical report or a conference paper for the material you need, although it is unlikely that someone will go to the trouble and expense of photocopying a thesis or dissertation and mailing it to you. If you have a more modest need, however, you will increase the likelihood of obtaining a favorable response if your request is precise and convincing. Most researchers are used to receiving requests for reprints (printed copies or photocopies of published articles), preprints (copies of manuscripts in press), and other information. But do not expect a busy researcher to answer a long list of questions or to send you material that is readily available in any college library.

If you are in a department that has many active researchers on the staff, it is possible that one of them is working on the very problem that interests you. To find out, ask your instructor, and also ask if it will be OK to approach that person. If the answer is yes, set up an appointment to discuss your interests, but be sure to do your homework on the topic first. List for yourself the questions you want to ask, and then take notes during the interview. You may be able to make a connection through the Internet with someone who knows something, but simply surfing the Net can be a real time waster.

Taking Notes in the Library

We have discussed retrieving abstracts and other material online and locating original material in the stacks, but not taking notes in the library. If you have the funds, the best way to ensure that your notes will be exact is to photocopy the material you need. But be sure to write down in a conspicuous place on the photocopy the complete citation of all you copied. You will still need to interpret what you copied, and it is often easier to make notes of your interpretation at the time you have the material in hand. Having such notes will enable you to write an accurate paper as well as one that is efficiently organized.

Making detailed notes will also help you avoid committing *plagiarism* accidentally. We will have more to say about this problem in Chapter Six, but you plagiarize intentionally when you knowingly copy or summarize someone's work without acknowledging that source. You plagiarize accidentally when you copy someone's work but forget to credit it or to put it in quotation marks. Plagiarism is illegal, and you should guard against it by keeping accurate notes and giving full credit to others when it is due.

If you are taking extensive notes on a laptop computer, you need some way to distance yourself from pages and pages of notes in order to bring coherence to them. The same would be true if you were taking handwritten notes in the library. A useful strategy with handwritten notes is to use a separate index card for each quotable idea that you find as you uncover relevant material in your literature search. Many writers prefer making notes on 5 × 8-inch index cards because they can usually get all the information they want on the front of a large card, so it is easier to find what they want later. If you are using a computer to take notes, you might print them out and then cluster them in logical batches (as you would large index cards). For each note, be sure to include the full reference of the material, including all the information you will need for the reference section of your paper, and the page numbers of verbatim quotes (to cite in the narrative of your paper).

If you have made an outline for an essay (as described in Chapter Four), you can code each card or printout with the particular section of the outline that the material on the card or printout will illustrate (or you can use color coding). An alternative is to use a folder for each section of your paper, and then to file the relevant batches in the appropriate folder. In this way, you can maintain a general order in your notes and avoid facing a huge stack of miscellaneous bits and pieces of information that will loom large as you try to sort and integrate them into a useful form. If you are using reference numbers to code material, be consistent, because a haphazard arrangement will only slow you down when it is time to write the first draft.

The most fundamental rule of note taking is to be thorough and systematic so that you do not waste time and energy having to return to the same book or article. Because memory is porous, it is better to photocopy or record too much than to rely on recall to fill in the gaps. Be sure your notes will make sense to you when you examine them later.

Source Credibility

Not all information is reliable, but the question is how to separate the credible from the suspect. This question is not easy to answer: A source of information that one person perceives as credible may not be perceived by another the same way. The way this problem is addressed in science is to subject manuscripts submitted to respected research journals to *peer review*, which means that editors send them out to experts in the same field for their independent evaluations and recommendations. It is not impossible, however, for even a poorly executed study to slip by occasionally, but as a general rule, researchers are taught to give greater weight to peer-reviewed journal articles than to unpublished manuscripts, technical reports, or chapters in edited books (which may be lightly reviewed, if at all). Textbooks are also sent out for review, but mostly because the prospective publisher wants to find out whether they will be saleable.

Even within the peer-reviewed literature, there is a pecking order of journals in any field. Manuscripts that are rejected by one journal might be sent to a second or third journal, until they finally find homes. This does not mean that articles in journals at the top of the pecking order are automatically more credible than those in other journals, but only that a social hierarchy of journals exists in every field, and the toughest journals in which to publish are usually those at the top of the social structure. In some cases, 85% or more of manuscripts submitted to the most prestigious journals are rejected by the editors based on peer reviews, although some manuscripts may be returned without review because in the editor's judgment they seemed to be inappropriate for that particular journal. A wise researcher, Yale psychologist Robert J. Sternberg, cautioned that "the place of publication is not a valid proxy for the quality and impact of the research" (*APA Observer*, October 2001, p. 40).

Some information is especially suspect, however, such as that in chat rooms on the Web. There is, in fact, a growing literature in psychological science on the nature of these chat rooms and the fertile ground they provide for rumor and gossip to take root. Because in a given instance it might be hard to decide whether something you read is a fact or a rumor (i.e., an unsupported allegation) or maybe even a boldfaced lie, the saying about "buying a pig in a poke" is applicable to much of this information. The best guidance we can give you is: When in doubt, ask your instructor for guidance.

Additional Tips

As you get started on the literature search, try to be realistic in assessing how much material you will need in your review. Too few journal articles or books may result in a weak foundation for your project, but too much material and intemperate expectations may overwhelm you and your topic. You are writing not a doctoral dissertation or an article for a journal but a required paper that must be completed within a limited amount of time. How can you find out what is a happy medium between too little and too much? Talk with your instructor before you start an intensive literature search. Ask whether your plan seems realistic.

Here are some more tips to get you started on the literature search and to do it efficiently:

- ◆ Before you start your literature search, ask the instructor to recommend any key works that you should read or consult. Even if you feel confident about your topic already, asking the instructor for specific leads can prevent your going off on a tangent.
- ◆ Do not expect to finish your literature search in one sitting. Students with unrealistic expectations make themselves overly anxious and rush a task that should be done patiently and methodically to achieve the best result.
- ◆ Suppose you cannot locate the original work that you are looking for in the stacks. Some students return repeatedly to the library, day after day, seeking a book or journal article before discovering that it has been lost or stolen or is being rebound. Ask an information librarian to find the elusive material. If the original work you need is unavailable, the librarian may consult another college library. However, the material could take so long to arrive that you might miss the deadline set by your instructor (this kind of delay is not an acceptable excuse).
- ◆ If you are looking for a specialized work, you probably will not find it in a small public library, so do not waste your time. When students spend a lot of time off-campus in public libraries and bookstores looking for source material, they usually come back with references from general texts or current mass-market books and periodicals, and these rarely constitute acceptable sources.
- ◆ Remember to keep a running checklist of the sources you searched and the search terms you used so that you don't accidentally retrace your steps.

Library Etiquette

Before we turn to the basics of developing your proposal for an essay or a research report, here is some final advice about using your library. The golden rule of library etiquette is to respect your library and remember that others also have to use it:

◆ Be quiet.
◆ Never tear pages out of journals or books.
◆ Never write in library journals or books.
◆ Do not monopolize material or machines.
◆ Return books and periodicals as soon as you finish with them.

3

DEVELOPING A PROPOSAL

Once you have chosen your topic, retrieved background work, and crystallized your ideas, the next step is to develop a proposal of what you plan to do. Some instructors feel that an oral presentation is sufficient, but most require a written proposal as a way of ensuring that both they and their students have a common understanding of the topic and the planned project, including all ethical issues.

Purpose of the Proposal

The object of your proposal is to tell the instructor what you would like to study. However, it is not simply a one-way communication, but an opportunity for the instructor to provide feedback and to raise questions that you need to address before going any further. If you are planning an empirical research study, the proposal is also usually an opportunity to anticipate and address any ethical concerns that might be raised. Thus, you might think of the proposal as a kind of "letter of agreement" between you and the instructor. Once the proposal has been formally approved, it is presumed that you will consult with the instructor before making changes in any aspect of the procedures or plan agreed upon.

Instructors may require preliminary submissions in addition to a written proposal. They may also ask for details in addition to those illustrated in the sample proposals in this chapter. The instructor may ask you how you arrived at your ideas and why you believe the topic is important and worth studying. The purpose of such questions is (a) to help you formulate your plans, (b) to encourage you to choose a topic you find intrinsically interesting, and (c) to make sure that these are *your* ideas. We will have more to say about the third point in Chapter Six, but it is essential that the work be your own even if it builds on, or is a replication of, previous work by others.

In fact, replication is regarded as an essential criterion of credible scientific knowledge because it continues the discovery process of science as it clarifies and expands the meanings and limits of hypotheses. Someone once compared the scientist to a person trying to unlock a door using a hitherto untried key. The role of replication, we might say, is to make the key available to others so they can see for themselves whether or not the key works in a particular situation. Replication does not mean merely reproducing a similar p value; it means observing a similar relationship or uncovering a similar phenomenon. Suppose you were out jogging one morning and spotted two Martians—not two people disguised as Martians, but real Martians: green skin, antennas poking out of their scalps, and all the rest. You are not going to whip out your calculator and perform a statistical test to see whether the p value is significant, but you sure are going to ask the nearest earthling, "Do you see what I see?" This is what replication in science is all about: You see for yourself what others have claimed to see. It is also why replications are often the basis of theses and course projects. However, the student is expected to add a creative touch to the design, in the form of a new hypothesis or some other innovative aspect.

The Essay Proposal

Exhibit 11 illustrates one form of the proposal for an essay, although your instructor may require another variation. This exhibit will at least get you thinking about what belongs in your proposal. Some things may need to be changed later, once you receive the instructor's feedback. It is clear that John's proposal did not come out of the blue, but that he met with the instructor even before drafting this proposal in order to get preliminary feedback.

Notice that John's name typed above each page beside the page number will serve as a safety device should any pages get accidentally detached. Some instructors prefer that students insert a page header (a couple of words from the title) rather than their names, as illustrated in the sample essay in Appendix A. The title is called a *working title* to reflect the idea that it can be changed later and is meant only to give an overall preview at this point.

John begins by describing the intention or goal of his planned essay. He tells where he wants to go and sketches his overall plan. He then mentions that he has retrieved some relevant work and tells how he expects to go forward from this starting point. The discussion is not vague but specifically mentions two reference databases (PsycINFO and AskERIC) and John's plan to use a third (*SSCI*). The proposal concludes with a preliminary list of references, which indicates that John has already put a lot of effort into the project.

EXHIBIT 11 *Sample proposal for an essay*

John Smith 1

Term Paper Proposal for Psychology 222

Submitted by John Smith

(Date the proposal is submitted)

Working Title

A Comparison of Two Theoretical Perspectives on Intelligence

Objective

I propose to contrast two major perspectives on the nature of human intelligence. One approach is the classic psychological assumption of a common factor in all measures of intelligence (called the g factor); theories that are consistent with this g-centered position have been dominant in psychology for many decades. In contrast to the classic approach is what I shall call the *multiplex view*, by which I mean the recent view asserting that many kinds of intelligences are housed within the same culture (like movies in a multiplex theater). In particular, I plan to focus on Howard Gardner's theory of multiple intelligences. I will explain his theory and also discuss some criticisms of it. Finally, I will give a flavor of what seems to be the direction of empirical research in this area.

Literature Search Strategy

I have started to search research databases and will continue to search PsycINFO, AskERIC, and other databases that are available online. I have already found some key books and will do an ancestry search using *SSCI,* using the published work of three major figures in the multiplex area (Howard Gardner, Robert Sternberg, and Steven Ceci) as my starting point. I will continue to consult

EXHIBIT 11   *Continued*

John Smith 2

with Professor Skleder concerning other possible leads and have already read the research on interpersonal acumen on which she collaborated. I have found useful an article written by a task force of the American Psychological Association (Neisser et al., 1996), have begun reading classic and recent books that are relevant to this topic, and have obtained a paper on interpersonal acumen by Dr. Ram N. Aditya and others (2000) that was presented at the American Psychological Society meeting (and have corresponded with him to request any further work).

Preliminary List of References

Aditya, R. N., Buboltz, W., Darkangelo, D., & Wilkinson, L. (2000, June). *Discriminant validation of a revised interpersonal acumen scale.* Paper presented at the meeting of the American Psychological Society, Miami, FL.

Ceci, S. J. (1990). *On intelligence...more or less: A bioecological treatise on intellectual development.* Englewood Cliffs, NJ: Prentice Hall.

Gardner, H. (1983). *Frames of mind: The theory of multiple intelligences.* New York: Basic Books.

Gardner, H. (1991). *The unschooled mind: How children think and how schools should teach.* New York: Basic Books.

Gardner, H. (1993). *Multiple intelligences: The theory in practice.* New York: Basic Books.

Herrnstein, R. J., & Murray, C. (1994). *The bell curve: Intelligence and class structure in American life.* New York: Free Press.

EXHIBIT 11   *Continued*

John Smith 3

Neisser, U., Boodoo, G., Bouchard, T. J., Jr., Boykin, A. W., Brody, N., Ceci, S. J.,

    Halpern, D. F., Loehlin, J. C., Perloff, R., Sternberg, R. J., & Urbina, S. (1996).

    Intelligence: Knowns and unknowns. *American Psychologist, 51,* 77-101.

Rosnow, R. L., Skleder, A. A., Jaeger, M. E., & Rind, B. (1994). Intelligence and the

    epistemics of interpersonal acumen: Testing some implications of Gardner's

    theory. *Intelligence, 19,* 93-116.

Spearman, C. (1927). *The abilities of man.* New York: Macmillan.

Sternberg, R. J. (1990). *Metaphors of mind: A new theory of human intelligence.*

    New York: Cambridge University Press.

Sternberg, R. J., & Detterman, D. K. (Eds.). (1986). *What is intelligence?*

    Contemporary viewpoints on its nature and definition. Norwood, NJ: Ablex.

Sternberg, R. J., & Wagner, R. K. (Eds.). (1986). *Practical intelligence: Nature and*

    origins of competence in the everyday world. New York: Cambridge University

    Press.

Thurstone, L. L. (1938). *Primary mental abilities.* Chicago: University of Chicago

    Press.

Thurstone, L. L., & Thurstone, T. G. (1941). *Factorial studies of intelligence.*

    (Psychometric Society Psychometric Monographs No. 2). Chicago: University

    of Chicago Press.

The Research Proposal

Exhibit 12 illustrates one form of a proposal for a research project. Jane describes the rationale of her hypotheses, the research design, how it will be implemented, how the data might be analyzed, and the question of ethical considerations. The more thorough Jane is, the more focused the instructor's comments can be, thus continuing the process of shepherding Jane toward her goal. It is evident that Jane has selected a topic that is of interest not only to her but also to the instructor, who has done research in this area.

If you plan to develop a questionnaire, put a preliminary verbal sketch of it in the proposal so the instructor can give you feedback with specific suggestions. Jane mentions that she has already gotten some guidance from the instructor about her proposed data analysis, and that she plans to discuss it with him again before deciding which of two strategies to use. She also discusses the ethics of the proposed research. The detail in the proposal reflects the considerable amount of time Jane has spent arriving at this stage and her consultations with the instructor on more than one occasion.

Ethical Considerations

Ethical accountability is, in fact, an important consideration in virtually every aspect of research. The absolute requirements of ethical accountability are (a) that you, the researcher, will protect the dignity, privacy, and safety of your participants and (b) that your research will be technically sound (so as not to waste precious resources, including the participants' time and effort) and not detrimental to society.

Here are some specific questions to get you thinking about the ethics of your proposed study:

- ◆ Might there be any psychological or physical risks to the participants? How do you plan to avoid these risks?
- ◆ Will any deception be used, and if so, is it really necessary, or can you think of a way to avoid using deception?
- ◆ How do you plan to debrief the participants? If you really must use a deception, then how do you plan to "dehoax" the deceived participants? How can you be sure that the dehoaxing procedure was effective?
- ◆ How do you plan to recruit the participants, and can you be sure that the recruitment procedure is noncoercive?
- ◆ How do you plan to use informed consent and to ensure that the participants understand that they are free to withdraw at any time without penalty?
- ◆ What steps will you take to ensure the confidentiality of the data?

EXHIBIT 12 *Sample proposal for a research study*

Jane Doe 1

Research Proposal for Psychology 333

Submitted by Jane Doe

(Date the proposal is submitted)

Working Title

An Experimental Investigation of the Effects of a Small Gift on Restaurant Tipping

Objective

An article by Lynn (1996) whetted my interest in the techniques that servers use to improve their tipping percentages, an area in which the instructor has done extensive research (Rind & Bordia, 1995, 1996). Many techniques seem to involve boosting the customers' impressions of the server's friendliness (e.g., a friendly touch or drawing a smiling face on the check). I propose to use another technique, and after discussing my idea with the instructor, I asked an acquaintance who owns a restaurant for permission to perform a study in which the server will present customers with a small gift (chocolate candy).

After reading an article by Regan (1971), I have also become interested in whether reciprocity (i.e., the idea that people feel obligated to return a favor) may further improve the effectiveness of this technique. I propose to manipulate this condition by having the server say, in an offhand manner, "Oh, have another piece of candy," which should create the impression that the candy favor is due to the server's (as opposed to the restaurant's) generosity. My prediction is that customers will feel obligated to return the server's favor by increasing the tips they give.

Altogether, I propose three hypotheses, which proceed on the assumption that the server's offer of candy will be perceived by customers as a gesture of friendliness. My first hypothesis is that the mere offer of the candy will have the

EXHIBIT 12   *Continued*

Jane Doe 2

effect of increasing tips when compared with a no-gift control condition. Second, I hypothesize that this effect is cumulative, so that offering two candies will stimulate tipping even more (compared with the control baseline). Third, proceeding from Regan's description of reciprocity, I hypothesize that creating the impression that the server is generous (as well as friendly) will stimulate the most tipping.

Proposed Method

The restaurant is an upscale Italian-American establishment in central New Jersey. I have gotten the owner's permission and have also described the proposed study to a female server, who has agreed to participate. I propose using a randomized design with the following four groups: (a) no candy condition, (b) 1 piece of candy condition, (c) 2 pieces of candy condition, and (d) 1 + 1 condition. I will write the condition on a card, shuffle the cards, and ask the server to draw (blindly) one card at a time. In the control condition, the instruction will be to present the check without offering any candy. In the 1-piece condition, the instruction will be to offer each customer in the dining party one piece of candy when presenting the check. In the 2-piece condition, the instruction will be to offer each customer two pieces of candy of the person's choice when presenting the check. In the 1 + 1 condition, the instruction will be to offer each customer one piece of candy and then state, "Oh, have another piece," as if it were a generous afterthought.

The server's interaction with customers in the dining party will be limited to the presentation of the check and the instructions on the randomly selected card. When the dining party leaves, the server will record privately on the same index card that was used to specify the treatment (a) the amount of the tip left by the party, (b) the amount of the bill before taxes, and (c) the party size. It should be possible to run 20 dining parties in each condition. This process will give me an equal number

EXHIBIT 12   *Continued*

Jane Doe 3

of cases (*n*) per condition, which is preferable to an unequal-*n* design because the more unequal the groups, the less the statistical power relative to an equal-*n* design with the same total sample size (*N*). In setting $N = 80$, I am assuming that this number will provide enough statistical power for me to detect medium-sized effects (*r* approximately .3) using *t* tests to compare conditions

Proposed Data Analysis

The dependent measure will be defined as the tip percentage—that is, the amount of the tip divided by the amount of the bill before taxes, which will then be multiplied by 100. I will begin by examining the basic descriptive data (means and variabilities), but I have not yet settled on the particular data analyses I will use to evaluate the hypotheses, as there are several possibilities based on the text. One possibility is simply to run *t* tests comparing each experimental group with the control, in which case I would expect the effect size *(r)* to be largest for the comparison of the 1 + 1 condition with the control condition and smallest for the comparison of the 1-piece condition with the control condition. Another idea is to perform a contrast analysis on all four conditions, which will allow me to evaluate the predicted increase in tipping as we go from control to 1-piece to 2-piece to 1 + 1 conditions. Also, if I start out by doing a one-way ANOVA on all four groups, I can use the mean square error (*MSE*) and denominator *df* of the overall *F* in my *t* tests comparing two conditions each. These ideas will be discussed with the instructor before I proceed with the data analysis.

Ethical Considerations

The study involves a mild deception in that the customers are unaware that they are participating in an experiment. I do not propose to debrief them because no potential risk is involved. I cannot ask people who are dining whether they will

EXHIBIT 12   *Continued*

agree to "participate in an experiment" because I would destroy the credibility of the
manipulation and render the study scientifically meaningless. The server and the
owner will be given full details of the results, and all tips will be the property of the
server.

Preliminary List of References

Department of Commerce. (1990). *Statistical abstracts of the United States.*
   Washington, DC: Author.

Lynn, M. (1996). Seven ways to increase servers' tips. *Cornell Hotel and Restaurant
   Administration Quarterly, 37*(3), 24-29.

Lynn, M., & Mynier, K. (1993). Effect of server posture on restaurant tipping.
   Journal of Applied Social Psychology, 23, 678-685.

McCall, M., & Belmont, H. J. (1995). *Credit card insignia and tipping: Evidence for
   an associative link.* Unpublished manuscript, Ithaca College.

Regan, D. T. (1971). Effects of a favor and liking on compliance. *Journal of
   Experimental Social Psychology, 7,* 627-639.

Rind, B., & Bordia, P. (1995). Effect of server's "thank you" and personalization on
   restaurant tipping. *Journal of Applied Social Psychology, 25,* 745-751.

Rind, B., & Bordia, P. (1996). Effect of restaurant tipping of male and female
   servers drawing a happy, smiling face on the backs of customers' checks.
   Journal of Applied Social Psychology, 26, 218-225.

Tempus Fugit

Because time flies when you are writing a required paper for a course, here are two final tips:

- ◆ Turn in your proposal on time. Instructors are also very busy people, and they (like you) schedule their work. Turning in a proposal late is like waving a red flag that signals the wrong message to your instructor. Instead of communicating that you are responsible and reliable and someone who thinks clearly, this red flag signals that you may be none of the above.
- ◆ Be precise. In Lewis Carroll's *Through the Looking Glass*, Alice (of *Alice in Wonderland*) comes upon Humpty Dumpty, who uses a word in a way that Alice says she does not understand. He smiles contemptuously and says, "Of course you don't—till I tell you. . . . When *I* use a word, it means just what I choose it to mean—neither more nor less." Unlike Humpty Dumpty, you do not have the luxury of telling your instructor to "take it or leave it." Nor do you have the extra time to keep resubmitting the proposal because you did not make the initial effort to be precise.

4

OUTLINING
THE ESSAY

*When you are ready to begin drafting your essay, the first step is
to create a rough outline. The imposition of form will help you
collect and refine your thoughts as you shape the paper, and
you can prepare a more detailed outline after you have thought
some more. But even if you do not outline before you begin the
first draft, you should at least do so afterward. If a logical, ordered
form does not emerge, the weak spots will become apparent and
you can fix them. (If you are writing a research report, you can
skip this chapter and go on to Chapter Five.)*

Where to Start

A weak structure or a lack of structure is a common flaw in students' essays. A
weak structure is a sure sign that the student did not develop an outline before
beginning to write—or even after drafting the paper. Without at least a rough
outline to work with, the first draft of the essay can ramble on endlessly, and
working with it becomes an exercise in shaking hands with an octopus. In contrast, if you have a rough outline, you know where your ideas and sentences
are heading. The more detailed the outline, the more organized the paper will
be and the more likely you are to complete it on time.

If done correctly, your outline will set down a logical progression of the
points of interest and, if you are writing an argumentative essay, the major arguments (and counterarguments) you want to present. You will be able to
produce a parallel construction of the text and a balanced hierarchy of organization. You can begin to prepare a tentative and general outline as you retrieve and read reference material. Use comparison and contrast as a way of
structuring the outline in your mind; then pull together facts, arguments, and
studies to document and expand on your subtopics.

Some students find it difficult to begin making even a rough outline. If you are having a problem getting started, there are three tricks you can try:

- Think of the outline as a miniaturized table of contents based on the headings and subheadings you might want to use in a particular section of your paper.
- Shop around for an interesting quote that encourages fresh thinking and, if it still seems relevant and pungent later on, can later launch the introduction as well as capture and focus the reader's interest.
- If you are writing an expository essay, ask yourself the reporter's questions: *who, what, when, where,* and *why.*

Before you begin writing (discussed in Chapter Six), you might want to revise or polish the preliminary outline so that it more precisely reflects the organizational structure of the first draft of your essay. Even this structure should be viewed not as carved in stone, but as something that can be molded to your ideas as they evolve. Use the structure to guide you, but do not be afraid to change it if your thinking changes.

The Rough Outline

The first outline you do can be simply a list of items you want to cover in your paper. You would then think about this list, put it aside for a day or so, and then think about it some more. Asking yourself the following questions should help you get going:

- How do I want to begin?
- What conclusions do I want to draw?
- What sections do I need between these two points?
- In each section, what do I want to emphasize?
- What illustrations, examples, or quotations can I use?
- What details do I use? In what order?

Turning to John Smith's essay in Appendix A, you can see that all of these questions are amply addressed in the sample paper. If you go back a couple of steps and ask how John began, you find that he might have sketched something like this in his first rough draft:

1. Point out that "intelligence" has different meanings in different contexts, and conclude the introduction with an overview of the rest of the paper.
2. Compare the traditional view of intelligence with the newer view, which I'll be calling the *multiplex view* of intelligence.
3. Emphasize Howard Gardner's theory of multiple intelligences, including his ideas on what defines a component of intelligence, what his seven kinds of intelligence are, and why he believes they are independent intellectual abilities.

4. Discuss the major criticisms of the newer view, and give some counter-arguments of these criticisms.
5. End by rehashing the point of the paper, noting its limitations, and saying something about the current or future direction of research.

There is enough here for John to begin to think about the fine details of each section and to frame a more meticulous outline. In getting down to specifics, he needs to keep all of his ideas parallel to ensure that there will be logical consistency in his arguments. Just as the preliminary outline can take different forms, the detailed outline can be set down in topics, sentences, or paragraphs—whichever seems to make the most sense as ideas begin to flow. The essential point is that these ideas are comparable or equivalent to one another—that is, parallel.

Making Ideas Parallel

Whether you decide to work with topics, sentences, or paragraphs, the specific form you choose should be the only one used in the outline. In the following outline fragment, the ideas are clearly not parallel:

I. What is intelligence? What does "*g*-centric" mean? What will follow?
II. Two views
    A. Traditional—the general overriding factor of intelligence is measured by every task on an intelligence test
    B. Spearman's psychometric contribution
    C. Developmental psychologists, following Piaget, argue for general mental structures
    D. The Bell Curve

The problem is that this outline is a hodgepodge of questions, topics, idea fragments, and a book title. Working with this jumble is like swimming upstream. Such an outline will only sabotage your efforts to put thoughts and notes into a logical sequence. Contrast this incoherent structure with the parallel structure of the following outline as it covers the section of John's essay called "Two General Conceptions of Intelligence":

I. Two views of intelligence
    A. The traditional approach
        1. General overriding trait (Spearman)
            a. "*g*-centric" notion of intelligence
            b. Jensen and heritability
        2. Piaget's idea of general structures of the mind
            a. Universal developmental sequence
            b. Biological operationalization (speed of neural transmission)
        3. Herrnstein and Murray's book on role of *g* in society

What makes the second outline superior to the first is not only that the same form is used throughout but that, in the second outline, the ideas are also logically ordered. The second outline looks more polished and inviting and will certainly be easier to use as a writing plan.

Putting Ideas in Order

To create this polished look, whether you use topics, sentences, or paragraphs for your outline, the trick is to try to group your information in descending order, from the most general facts or ideas to the most specific details and examples. You can see this approach clearly in the parallel format of the outline shown immediately above.

The rule of orderly precision applies whether you are outlining definitions, the nature of a particular theory, evaluation criteria, or a series of arguments and counterarguments. You can see the order and precision in the following outline segment:

II. Gardner's theory of "intelligences"
   A. Definition of intelligence
      1. Problem solving and creative abilities
      2. Evaluation criteria
         a. Isolation if brain-damaged
         b. Existence of exceptional populations
         c. Unique core operations
         d. Distinctive developmental history
         e. Existence of primitive antecedents
         f. Openness to experimentation
         g. Prediction of performance on tests
         h. Accessibility of information content
   B. Kinds of intelligence
      1. Logical-mathematical
      2. Linguistic
      3. Spatial
      4. Bodily-kinesthetic
      5. Musical
      6. Personal
         a. Intrapersonal
         b. Interpersonal

Another convention in making a detailed outline, as illustrated in Exhibit 13, is that if there is a subtopic division, there should be at least two subtopics, never only one. Facts, ideas, and concepts are classified by the use of roman numerals I, II, III; capitals A, B, C; arabic numerals 1, 2, 3; small letters a, b, c; and finally numbers and letters in parentheses. Thus, if you list I, you should list II (and perhaps III and IV and so on); if A, then B; if 1, then 2.

EXHIBIT 13   *Subdivision of the outline*

I.
  A.
  B.
     1.
     2.
        a.
        b.
           (1)
           (2)
              (a)
              (b)
II.

The roman numerals indicate the outline's main ideas. Indented capital letters provide main divisions within each main idea. The letters and numbers that follow list the supporting details and examples. Note the indentation of each subtopic. Any category can be expanded to fit the number of supporting details or examples that you wish to cover in the paper. Any lapses in logic are bound to surface if you use this system of organization, so you can catch and correct them before proceeding.

For example, look at the following abbreviated outline; Item B is clearly a conspicuous lapse in logic:

> II. Gardner's theory of "intelligences"
>   A. His definition of intelligence
>   B. How did the concept of *g* originate?
>   C. Seven kinds of intelligence

Item B should be moved from this section of the outline to the one pertaining to the *g*-centric view of intelligence. Some items may require a return to the library to clarify a point or to supplement parts of the outline with additional reference material.

Template for Writing and Note Taking

The outline is a way not only to organize your thoughts but also to make it easier to start writing. If you use the phrase or sentence format, the paper will almost write itself, as we see clearly in the following outline fragment:

> II. Gardner's theory of "intelligences"
>   A. Definition of intelligence

    1. " . . . the ability to solve problems, or to create products
that are valued within one or more cultural settings"
(Gardner, 1983, p. x)

    2. Intellectual talent must satisfy eight criteria (Gardner, 1983)

        a. Possible identification of intelligences by damage to particular areas of the brain

        b. Existence of exceptional populations (savants), implying
the distinctive existence of a special entity

Had our hypothetical outline used complete sentences, the paper would write itself:

  II. Gardner's theory of "intelligences"

    A. Definition of intelligence

      1. Gardner (1983) conceived of intelligence as "the ability to
solve problems, or to create products that are valued within
one or more cultural settings" (p. x).

      2. Gardner (1983) argued that a talent must fit eight criteria to
be considered "intelligence."

        a. There is potential to isolate the intelligence by brain
damage.

        b. Exceptional populations (e.g., savants) provide evidence
of distinct entities.

In Chapter Two, we alluded to one other helpful hint about preparing an outline. The outline's coding system makes it convenient to code the notes you take during your literature search. If your notes refer to section "II.B.1" of your outline, then you would record this code on the card, photocopy, or computer printout. In this way, order is brought to your notes. If you are using cards, for example, you can spread them on a large table and sort through them according to the section from your notes and the outline, each component enhancing the other.

Keep in mind, however, that the outline is only a guide. Its specific structure may change as you integrate your notes.

Outlining After the Fact

Some students write their papers over more than one semester (a senior thesis, for example) and may feel they cannot outline from the outset because they do not know where the final paper will go. When they do sit down to write, they tend to incorporate material from their earlier drafts, but they do not make an outline first. Still other students find the process of making an outline too exacting, preferring instead to sit at a word processor and let the stream of ideas flow spontaneously.

If either case describes you, then be sure to outline after the fact. To assure yourself that your work has an appealing, coherent form—what psychologists call a "good Gestalt"—make a "mini-table-of-contents" of your final draft, and then do a more detailed outline within the headings and subheadings. Ask yourself:

- ◆ Is the discussion focused, and do the ideas flow from or build on one another?
- ◆ Is there ample development of each idea?
- ◆ Are there supporting details for each main idea discussed?
- ◆ Are the ideas balanced?
- ◆ Is the writing to the point, or have I gone off on a tangent?

An experienced writer working with a familiar topic might be able to achieve success without a detailed outline. But for others, the lack of an outline often creates havoc and frustration, not to mention wasted time and effort. If you would like to practice on someone else's work, try outlining some section of John Smith's paper in Appendix A. Ask yourself how well his discussion addresses the five preceding questions. If you find problems with the structure of his discussion, think of ways he could have avoided them or corrected them before submitting the final draft.

5

PLANNING THE RESEARCH REPORT

The basic structure and form of research reports in psychology have evolved over many years. In this chapter, we describe this structure and form in the context of the sample report in Appendix B. A knowledge of these matters will enable you to organize your thoughts and plan the first draft (discussed in the next chapter). (If you are writing an essay, you can skip this chapter and go on to Chapter Six.)

The Basic Structure

Research methods texts routinely cover data collection and data analysis, and we will assume that you are mastering those techniques. What remains is to develop a research report that will explain in clear language (a) what you did, (b) why you did it, (c) what you found out, (d) what your findings mean, and (e) what you have concluded. Well-written reports imply a logical progression in thought, and by adhering to the structure described in this chapter, you can create this kind of order in your finished paper.

Looking again at Jane Doe's report in Appendix B, we see that it consists of eight parts:

Title page
Abstract
Introduction
Method
Results
Discussion
References
End material (tables and appendix)

Except for the layout of the title page and the addition of an appendix in Jane's report, the basic structure corresponds to a standard reporting format that has evolved over many years in psychology. Later on, we will discuss the layout of the paper, but you can see that the title page is straightforward; so let us focus on the parts that remain.

Abstract

Although the abstract (or synopsis) appears at the beginning of your report, it is actually written after the paper is completed. The abstract provides a concise summary of your report. Think of it as a distillation into one succinct paragraph of the important points covered in the body of the report. In the sample research report, Jane summarizes what she did, what she found, and what she concluded.

When planning your abstract, answer these questions as concisely as possible:

- What was the objective or purpose of my research study?
- What principal method did I use?
- Who were the research participants?
- What were my major findings?
- What did I conclude from these findings?

More detailed and more specific statements about methods, results, and conclusions are given in the body of your report. The abstract is presented first, and its purpose is to let the reader anticipate what your report is about.

Introduction

The introduction provides the rationale for your research and prepares the reader for the methods you have chosen. Thus, you should give a concise history and background of your topic, leading into your hypotheses or questions. In her opening paragraph, Jane cites a demographic finding and notes its implications for the importance of her topic; she goes on to summarize the relevant results of previous research on the topic. In this way, she underscores the value of her research as well as develops a logical foundation for her hypotheses.

Your literature review shows the development of your hypotheses or exploratory questions and the reason(s) the research topic seemed worth studying. Strong introductions are those that state the research problem or the hypotheses in such a way that the method section appears to be a natural consequence of that statement. If you can get readers to think when they later see your method section, "Yes, of course, that's what this researcher had to do to answer this question," then you will have succeeded in writing a strong introduction. Here are some questions to ask yourself as you plan the introduction:

- What was the purpose of my study?
- What terms need to be defined?

◆ How does my study build on or derive from other studies?
◆ What were my hypotheses, predictions, or expectations?

Method

The next step is to detail the methods and procedures used. If you used research participants, you should describe them (for example, the age, sex, and number of participants, as well as the way they were selected and any other details that will help to identify them specifically). Psychologists are trained to ask questions about the generalizability of research results. Your instructor will be thinking about the generalizability of your findings across both persons and settings (that is, the *external validity* of your results). If your participants were college students, the instructor may ask whether your results can be generalized beyond this specialized population.

Also included in this section should be a description of any tests or measures and the context in which they were used. Even if you used well-known, standardized tests, it is still a good idea to describe them in a few sentences. By describing them, you tell the instructor that you understand the nature and purpose of the instruments you used.

For instance, suppose you used the Self-Monitoring Scale developed by psychologist Mark Snyder (see "Self Monitoring of Expressive Behavior," *Journal of Personality and Social Psychology*, 1974, vol. 30, pp. 526–537). In your literature search, you found that research has shown this instrument to be three-dimensional (see "An Analysis of the Self-Monitoring Scale," by S. R. Briggs, J. M. Cheek, and A. H. Buss, *Journal of Personality and Social Psychology*, 1980, vol. 38, pp. 679–686). In your report, you might say something like:

> The study participants were administered Snyder's (1974) 25-item Self-Monitoring Scale. The original purpose of this instrument was to measure self-control and self-observation, but Briggs, Cheek, and Buss (1980) found that the scale actually measures three distinct factors, described by them as extraversion, other-directedness, and acting. *Extraversion* refers to the tendency to be the center of attention in groups; *other-directedness*, to a person's willingness to change his or her behavior to suit others; and *acting*, to liking and being good at speaking and entertaining.

However, suppose you need to report only the nature of a particular measure and not any follow-up inferences by other researchers. For example, assume you used the Need for Cognition Scale created by social psychologists John T. Cacioppo and Richard E. Petty (see "The Need for Cognition," *Journal of Personality and Social Psychology*, 1982, vol. 42, pp. 116–131). You can succinctly describe the measure in a single sentence:

> The participants were administered Cacioppo and Petty's (1982) Need for Cognition Scale, which is an 18-item measure of the tendency to engage in and enjoy thinking.

If you know something about the reliability and validity of the instrument, mention this information as well (along with an appropriate citation), but be specific. For example, it would be vague to say only that "the reliability was $r = 50$" without also indicating whether you mean the *test-retest reliability* (i.e., the stability of the instrument from one measurement session to another), the *alternate form reliability* (i.e., the degree of equivalence of different versions of the instrument), the *internal-consistency reliability* (i.e., the degree of relatedness of individual items or components of the instrument when those items or components are used to give a single score), or another form of reliability. The same rule applies to the reporting of validity findings; tell which type of validity you mean of those described in Exhibit 14.

Results

In the next major section, describe your findings. You might plan to show the results in a table, as in the sample report in Appendix B, or in a figure (a bar chart or a frequency polygon, for example). Do not make the reader guess what you are thinking; label your table or figure fully, and discuss the data in the narrative text so that it is clear what they represent. It is not necessary to repeat the results from the table or figure in your narrative; simply tell what they mean.

Ask yourself the following questions as you structure your results section:

◆ What did I find?
◆ How can I say what I found in a careful, detailed way?
◆ Is what I am planning to say precise and to the point?
◆ Will what I have said be clear to the reader?
◆ Have I left out anything of importance?

This section should consist of a careful, detailed analysis that strikes a balance between being discursive and being falsely or needlessly precise:

◆ You are guilty of *false precision* when something inherently vague is presented in overly precise terms. Suppose you used a standard attitude measure in your research, and suppose the research participants responded on a 5-point scale from "strongly agree" to "strongly disagree." It would be falsely precise to report the means to a high number of decimal places, because your measuring instrument was not that sensitive to slight variations in attitudes.
◆ You are guilty of *needless precision* when (almost without thinking about it) you report something much more exactly than the circumstances require. For example, reporting the weight of mouse subjects to six decimal places might be within the bounds of your measuring instrument, but the situation does not call for such exactitude.

The rule of thumb in reporting test statistics (such as the *t* test, the *F* test, and the chi-square), effect-size indices (such as Cohen's *d*, Hedges's *g*, and the

EXHIBIT 14   *Uses of the term validity in research and assessment*

---

construct validity: the degree to which the measuring instrument is a gauge of the variable or characteristic of interest.

content validity: the extent to which the measuring instrument represents the content area it is supposed to represent.

convergent validity: validity that is supported by a substantial correlation of conceptually similar measures.

criterion validity: the degree to which the measuring instrument correlates with one or more outcome criteria (also called *criterion variables*).

discriminant validity: validity supported by a lack of correlation between conceptually unrelated measures

external validity: the degree of generalizability.

inferential validity: causal inferences made in a laboratory setting that are applicable to events they were meant to apply to beyond the laboratory.

internal validity: the degree of validity of statements made about whether X causes Y.

predictive validity: the extent to which the measuring instrument can predict future outcomes.

statistical conclusion validity: the relative accuracy of drawing statistical conclusions.

Pearson r), and measures of central tendency (means, medians, and modes) and variability (standard deviations and variances) is to round to two decimal places. But in calculating the results, it is a good idea not to scrimp on the number of decimal places in the intermediate calculations. Suppose you are a NASA engineer trying to figure out how much fuel will be needed to complete a mission to Mars. If you round the calculations, you might send the astronauts on an impossible mission. Also, in reporting effect sizes, do not just say "the effect size was .25" without indicating which measure of effect size you are referring to, because it makes a big difference whether the .25 refers to the standardized difference between two groups (i.e., Cohen's d or Hedges's g) or to the point-biserial correlation (r_{pb}) between group membership and the participants' individual scores on the dependent variable.

Another convention that many students find confusing is the way that p values are to be presented. Many statisticians recommend reporting the actual descriptive level of significance, because it carries more information than the phrases "significant difference" or "no significant difference at the 5% level." Assuming your instructor does not frown on reporting p values to more than two decimal places, you have several options. One possibility is to list a string of zeros, such as "$p = .00000025$." Another alternative is to use scientific notation as a more compact way to show a very small p value. That is, instead of reporting $p = .00000025$, you report 2.5^{-7}, where -7 tells the reader to count 7 places to the left of the decimal in 2.5 and make that the decimal place. Of course, if you are looking up p values in a statistical table, you may not have the option of reporting them precisely. Thus, another choice is to state only that p is less than (<) or greater than (>) the particular column value in the statistical table.

When reporting p values in tables, the convention is to use a notation system of asterisks for two-tailed p values and daggers (or some other symbol) for one-tailed p values. For instance, if you wanted to indicate that significance values were ".05 or less two-tailed," you would use one asterisk; if they were ".01 or less two-tailed," you would use two asterisks, and so on. However, whatever option you use, the essential point is not to confuse "nonsignificance" with "no effect." If there really is no effect (i.e., the effect size is zero), then the expected value of the t statistic equals 0, the F statistic usually is approximately 1, and the chi-square (χ^2) statistic equals the degrees of freedom (df) of the χ^2.

Incidentally, a common mistake in reporting ratings and attitudinal scores using 5-point scales is that they are often mistakenly called "Likert scales." Technically, a *Likert scale* (named after Rensis Likert, its inventor) means that the items on the scale were selected by a particular method (called *summated ratings* by Likert). But this is not what most researchers really mean when they say they used a Likert scale. Some researchers skirt this problem by using the term "Likert-type scale," by which they merely mean that the response alternatives were accompanied by phrases or words (for example, "very favorable," "favorable," "neutral," "unfavorable," and "very unfavorable"), but they did not use the method of summated ratings to develop the scale. If this is all you mean, you can simply say something like "The response scale ranged from 'very favorable' (1) to 'very unfavorable' (5)."

Discussion

In the discussion section, you will form a cohesive unit from the facts you have gathered. A review of the introductory section is often helpful. Think about how you will discuss your research findings in light of how you framed your hypotheses in your proposal. Did serendipity play a role in your study? If so, detail the unexpected by-products and ideas.

Try to write "defensively" without being too blatant about it. That is, be your own devil's advocate and ask yourself what a skeptical reader might see as the other side of your argument or conclusion. In particular, look for shortcomings or critical inconsistencies, and anticipate the reader's reaction to them. If you cannot find any holes in your argument or conclusion, ask a clever friend to help you out by listening to your argument.

Here are some additional questions to consider as you begin to structure this section:

◆ What was the purpose of my study?
◆ How do my results relate to that purpose?
◆ Were there any serendipitous findings of interest?

- How valid and generalizabable are my findings?
- Are there larger implications in these findings?
- Is there an alternative way to interpret my results?

If you believe there are larger implications of your research findings, the discussion section is the place to spell them out. Are there implications for further research? If so, propose them here. In Appendix B, in her final paragraph, Jane suggests ideas for future research.

Incidentally, some researchers add a separate conclusions section when they want to separate the ideas and arguments in the discussion from some pithy conclusions. However, it is quite proper to treat the final paragraph of your discussion section as the place for your conclusions. In either case, your conclusions should be stated as clearly and precisely as possible.

References

Once you have made plans for writing the body of the report, give some thought to your reference material again. You will need to include an alphabetized listing of all the sources of information you drew from, and it is essential that virtually every citation (not personal communications, for example) be listed in your references section. To avoid retracing your steps in the library, keep a running list of the material that will appear in this section as you progress through the early preparation of the report. You can create a separate file called "References" and then copy and paste them into your paper's references section. If at the last minute you suddenly find you need to recheck the author, title, or publisher of a particular book, remember that you can go to your library's automated catalog.

End Material

The APA publication manual stipulates that tables and figures be placed in the manuscript after the references section, which is a convenience for the copyeditor and the printer. The report in Appendix B follows this style, as many instructors prefer students use it. However, since your paper is not being submitted for publication, your instructor may permit you to insert tables and figures within the narrative section of your paper; this is easy enough to do if you are using a standard word-processing program. The APA manual also requires that footnotes to the narrative text be on a separate page immediately after the references section and before any tables or figures, another convenience for the printer of journal articles. Not all instructors insist on this format, and you should check with your instructor if you have a question about how to proceed (ask whether it is OK to let your word-processing program automatically insert footnotes at the bottom of the relevant pages).

Most instructors like to see the raw materials and computations of the investigation. This information can be prepared as an appendix at the end of your report or as a separate package of materials. Our preference, as illustrated in the sample report, is to place this information at the end of the paper in an appendix. Had Jane used a lengthy test or questionnaire that did not belong in the limited space of the method section, she would have included it in the appendix of her report. Assuming your instructor would like to see your calculations, you can describe what you did in the appendix, as Jane does. If you used a statistical program to analyze your data, you can make a printout, pare it down to essentials, and include the pared-down results as an appendix in your paper.

Whether or not your instructor requires an appendix (or stipulates a different list of items to be included), it is very important that you keep all your notes and data until the instructor has returned your report and you have received a grade in the course—just in case the instructor has questions about your work.

Organizing Your Thoughts

In the preceding chapter we described the way to create an outline for the essay. The research report does not require a gross outline because its formal structure already provides a skeleton waiting to be fleshed out. Nevertheless, all researchers find it absolutely essential to organize their thoughts about each section before writing the first draft. There are three ways to do this:

◆ If you would like to learn about outlining, Chapter Four provides guidelines on how to outline before or after the fact.
◆ You can make notes on separate index cards for each major point (for example, the rationale of the study, the derivation of each hypothesis, and each background study) and draw on these notes to write your first draft.
◆ You can simply make a computer file of such notes.

If you are still having a hard time getting going, here are two more tips:

◆ Imagine you are sitting across a table from a friend; tell your "friend" what you found.
◆ Take a tape recorder for a walk; tell it what you found in your research.

No matter what approach you favor, make sure that your notes or files are accurate and complete. If you are summarizing or paraphrasing something you read, you must note the full citation. If you are quoting someone, include the statement in quotation marks and make sure that you have copied it exactly.

6

WRITING AND
REVISING

Writing a first draft is a little like taking the first dip in chilly ocean waters on a hot day. It may be uncomfortable at the outset but feels better once you get used to it. In this chapter, we provide some pointers to buoy you up as you begin writing. We also provide tips to help you revise your work.

Sorting Through Your Material

Back in 1947, there was a fascinating story in newspapers and magazines about two brothers, the Collyers, who were found dead in a rubbish-filled mansion at Fifth Avenue and 128th Street in New York City. On receiving a tip that one brother, Homer Collyer, had died, the police forced their way into the mansion with crowbars and axes. They found all of the entrances to the house blocked by wrapped packages of newspapers, hundreds of cartons and all kinds of junk (14 grand pianos, most of a Model-T Ford, the top of a horse-drawn carriage, a tree limb 7 feet long and 20 inches in diameter, an organ, a trombone, a cornet, three bugles, five violins, three World War I bayonets, and 10 clocks, including one 9 feet high and weighing 210 pounds). The rooms and hallways were honeycombed with tunnels through all this debris and booby-trapped so that anything disturbed would come crashing down on an intruder. The police began searching for the other brother, Langley, who had been caring for Homer, as it was thought that he might have phoned in the tip. After 8 weeks of burrowing through the incredible mess, they finally found the body of Langley Collyer wedged between a chest of drawers and a bedspring, killed by one of his own booby traps.

For students writing essays and research reports, the lesson of the Collyer brothers is that it is not always easy to discard things you have made an effort to save, including notes, studies, and quotes that you have gone to the trouble to track down. But quantity cannot replace quality and relevance in the material you save for your research report or essay. Instructors are more impressed

59

by tightly reasoned papers than by ones that are overflowing with superfluous material. It is best to approach the writing and revising stage with an open but focused mind—that is, a mind that is focused on the objective but that is at the same time open to discarding irrelevant material (not research data, however).

The Self-Motivator Statement

To begin the first draft, write down somewhere for yourself the purpose or goal you have in mind (that is, what your paper will be about). Keep this "self-motivator statement" brief so that you have a succinct focus for your thoughts as you begin to enter them into your word processor or set them down on paper. On the assumption that you consulted your instructor and afterward jotted down ideas you spoke about, you can draw on these notes to help you write your self-motivator statement.

If we refer to the two papers at the end of this book, we can imagine the following self-motivators after the students had consulted with their instructors, thought about their notes, and formulated an overall plan on how to proceed:

From John Smith

I'm going to compare the *g*-centered view of intelligence with what I am going to term the *multiplex view* because the way that different abilities are subsumed under the term *intelligence* reminds me of how different movies are housed together in a multiplex theater. I will emphasize Howard Gardner's theoretical approach, the criticisms, and the counterarguments. At the end, I will try to say something about both current and future directions of research on intelligence.

From Jane Doe

I'm going to describe how I found that tipping increases when people are given a small gift, and how the manipulation of a reciprocity effect can further increase tipping. I will begin with a background review that puts my hypotheses in context, and I will conclude with some reservations and ideas for further research.

As you can see, this trick of using a self-motivator statement can help to concentrate your thoughts. It should also make the task of writing seem less formidable. The self-motivator is a good way simply to get you going and keep you clearheaded, and it is also a good way to filter out material that can be discarded. You will be less apt to go off on a tangent if every once in a while you glance at this statement to remind yourself of your plan for the paper's direction.

The Opening

A good opening is crucial if the reader's attention and interest are to be engaged. Some writers are masters at creating good openings, but many technical articles and books in psychology start out ponderously. There are certainly enough cases of ponderous writing so that we need not give examples. But what about openings that grip our minds and make us want to delve further into the work?

One technique for beginning a paper in an inviting way is to pose a stimulating question. For example, psychologist Sissela Bok wrote a book about the ethics of lying, ostensibly a pretty dry and uninviting subject to many people, but opened her book (*Lying: Moral Choice in Public and Private Life*, Pantheon, 1978) with a number of compelling questions that resonate with immediacy and vibrancy:

> Should physicians lie to dying patients so as to delay the fear and anxiety which the truth might bring them? Should professors exaggerate the excellence of their students on recommendations in order to give them a better chance in a tight job market? Should parents conceal from children the fact that they were adopted? Should social scientists send investigators masquerading as patients to physicians in order to learn about racial and sexual biases in diagnosis and treatment? Should government lawyers lie to Congressmen who might otherwise oppose a much-needed welfare bill? And should journalists lie to those from whom they seek information in order to expose corruption? (p. xv)

By posing these questions, the author speaks to readers in the same way that she would if she were opening a dialogue. If we think about the questions, even for a moment, we are compelled to answer them, even if only subconsciously. We are drawn into the book because we want to compare Bok's answers to her questions with our own thinking.

Another technique is to try to rivet attention by impressing on readers the paradoxical nature of a timely issue. In *Obedience to Authority* (Harper, 1969), social psychologist Stanley Milgram began as follows:

> Obedience is as basic an element in the structure of social life as one can point to. Some system of authority is a requirement of all communal living, and it is only the man dwelling in isolation who is not forced to respond, through defiance or submission, to the commands of others. Obedience, as a determinant of behavior, is of particular relevance to our time. It has been reliably established that from 1933 to 1945 millions of innocent people were systematically slaughtered on command. Gas chambers were built, death camps were guarded, daily quotas of corpses were produced with the same efficiency as the manufacture of appliances. These inhumane policies may have originated in the mind of a single person, but they could only have been carried out on a massive scale if a very large number of people obeyed orders. (p. 1)

Milgram's passage first stirs our imagination because it reminds us that obedience is a basic part of social life. What ultimately draws us into Milgram's book is the matter-of-fact way he refers to the grotesque nature of the Holocaust, letting the deadly facts speak for themselves. He leads us to a logical conclusion, setting the stage for the rest of his thesis. Incidentally, this passage was written before there were concerns about sexist language: Milgram's use of the word *man* ("it is only the man dwelling in isolation") as a general term for men and women is now considered improper usage. Instead, he could have said "the person dwelling in isolation" (we return to this issue later).

However, perhaps you are thinking, "What does Milgram's or Bok's work have to do with me? These are Ph.D. psychologists who were writing for publication, but I'm just writing a paper for a course." The answer any instructor will give you is that an expectation of good writing that captures the reader's attention and draws the reader into the message is not limited to published work. It also applies, for instance, to correspondence in businesses and organizations, company memos, and applications for jobs.

In the sample papers at the end of this book, what makes the opening passages inviting is that they also strike a resonant chord in the reader. There are many other useful opening techniques. A definition, an anecdote (for example, the strange case of the Collyer brothers), a metaphor that compares or contrasts (such as using *the Collyer brothers* as a synonym for "pack rats"), an opening quotation (called an *epigraph*), and so on—all of these are devices that a writer can use to shape a beginning paragraph. Not only should the opening lead the reader into the work, but it should also provide momentum for the writer as the words begin to flow. John Smith begins his essay by implying a paradox, which is that we ordinarily speak of "intelligence" in many different ways, but psychologists have traditionally viewed it in one general way. Jane Doe's research report starts with interesting facts, which immediately lead us into the logic of her introduction, and ultimately to her hypotheses.

Settling Down to Write

Should you find yourself still having trouble beginning the introductory section, try the trick of not starting with the introductory paragraph. Start writing whatever paragraph or section you feel will be the easiest, and then tackle the rest as your ideas begin to flow. When faced with a blank computer screen and a flashing cursor, some students escape by surfing the Net, playing video games, taking a nap, or wandering around to find somebody to chat with. Recognize these and similar counterproductive moves for what they are, because they can drain your energies. Use them instead as rewards *after* you have done a good job of writing.

The following are general pointers to ensure that your initial writing will go as smoothly as possible:

- While writing, try to work in a quiet, well-lighted place in 2-hour stretches (dim lighting makes people sleepy). Even if you are under time pressure to finish the paper quickly, it is important to take a break so you can collect your thoughts and make sure you are not writing aimlessly or drifting off in a wrong direction.
- When you take a break, go for a stroll, preferably outside, because the fresh air will be invigorating, and the change of environment will help you think about what you have already written and what you want to say next.
- If you are unexpectedly called away while you are in the middle of an idea, jot down a phrase or a few words that will get you back on the track once you return to your writing. (Be sure to save your work before you leave.)
- When you stop for the day, try to stop at a point that is midway through a thought that you are finding difficult to express or complete. When you wake up the next day, your mind will be fresh with new ideas, and your writing will not have to start cold.
- Try to pace your work with time to spare so that you can complete the first draft and let it rest for a day. When you return to the completed first draft after a night's sleep, your critical powers will be enhanced, and you will have a fresh approach to shaping the final draft.

Ethics of Writing and Reporting

The most fundamental ethical principle in scholarly writing is honesty in all aspects of the work. If you are conducting empirical research and writing a report, this principle means honesty in all aspects of the project, from its implementation to your public account of the procedures that you used, your findings, their limitations, and their plausible implications. Two prime examples of deliberate dishonesty are the falsification of data and the fabrication of results, which constitute fraud. In the same way that the professional career of a researcher who falsifies data or fabricates results is compromised, the consequences will be harsh for the student writing a research report in which the data or results are fabricated.

Knowingly misrepresenting the implications of actual findings is also unethical, whether it involves what Robert Rosenthal has called *hyperclaiming* (i.e., exaggerating the implications of research) or *causism* (i.e., falsely implying a causal relationship). For example, using expressions such as "the effect of," "the impact of," "the consequence of," and "as a result of" clearly implies that there is a causal relationship. But if the research design does not allow you to make a causal inference, you are guilty of hyperclaiming by using this language. To avoid this problem, simply use the appropriate language, including expressions like "was related to," "was predictable from," or "could be inferred from." As Rosenthal has argued, if the perpetrator is aware of the problem, then the causism reflects blatant unethical misrepresentation and deception; if the perpetrator is unaware, then it reflects ignorance or lazy writing.

Honesty in research reporting and other scholarly writing also means giving credit where credit is due. For students, this means that if the instructor, a teaching assistant, or someone else helped you in some significant way, you acknowledge that contribution in your narrative or in a footnote. For example, Jane mentions in her results section that she consulted with the instructor regarding two data-analytic approaches and chose one only after discussing it with the instructor. Should your research later become part of an article authored by your instructor, the decision as to whether you will be listed as a coauthor or in a footnote acknowledgment will depend on the nature of your contribution to the research. Analyzing data that the instructor provided may be a minor contribution deserving a footnote acknowledgment, but if the article is substantially based on your individual efforts (as in a dissertation or a senior honors thesis), you will usually be listed as a coauthor, possibly even as the principal author, depending on the extent of your contribution.

Another important ethical standard concerns the sharing of data with those who want to verify published claims by reanalyzing the results. Provided that the confidentiality of the study participants is protected, and unless legal rights preclude the release of the data, psychologists are expected to make their empirical findings available to other competent professionals. Instructors have the option to require students writing research reports to provide the raw data on which the work is based. If confidentiality is a potential problem, ask the instructor how the data should be coded to protect the privacy of those who have participated in your study.

Before we turn to what many instructors consider the most significant concern in student papers—the avoidance of plagiarism—we will mention one further standard with implications for students. It is unethical to misrepresent as fresh data any research results that have already been published or reported. If the data have already been published or reported elsewhere, the researcher is expected to say so and to tell where. The reason for this rule is to avoid causing research consumers to mistakenly believe that a separate report of the same research findings implies that the research has been successfully replicated. The implication for psychology students is that it is unacceptable to submit the same work for additional credit in different courses. It may be acceptable to base the literature review in a research report for one course on the more extensive review in a paper for another course, but only with the full knowledge and consent of the instructors.

Avoiding Plagiarism

The most nagging concern of most instructors who teach writing-intensive courses in psychology is conveying the meaning and consequences of plagiarism. The term *plagiarism*, which comes from the Latin word meaning "kidnapper," refers to the theft of another person's ideas or work and passing it off as your own. It is crucial that you understand what constitutes plagiarism and be aware that the penalties can be severe. Claiming not to know that you committed plagiarism is not an acceptable defense. Simply stated, stealing someone else's work and passing it off as your own is wrong, and even if it is "accidental" or unintentional, the penalty in a class assignment or a thesis may be harsh.

In fact, it is easy to avoid committing plagiarism. All you must be is attentive and willing to make the effort to paraphrase the passage in question (and cite the source exactly), or else quote the passage word for word and put quotation marks around it (and, of course, cite the source and page number). If the passage is lengthy (40 or more words), as illustrated by the two passages that we quoted previously from Bok's and Milgram's books, then quotation marks are not used; instead the passage is set off as a *block quotation* (indented about ½ inch from the left margin, with the page number indicated in parentheses after the final period).

To illustrate plagiarism and how easily it can be avoided, assume that a student writing an essay came across Sissela Bok's book on lying and copied down the following passage for future reference:

> Deceit and violence—these are two forms of deliberate assault on human beings. Both can coerce people into acting against their will. Most harm that can befall victims through violence can come to them also through deceit. But deceit controls more subtly, for it works on belief as well as action. Even Othello, whom few would have dared to try to subdue by force, could be brought to destroy himself and Desdemona through falsehood. (Bok, 1978, p. 18)

There would be no problem if the student reproduced this passage just as it appears here, because the student has copied the passage accurately and has properly noted the page on which it appeared. The plagiarism problem would arise if the student decided to change a word or two to make the passage sound a little different and then passed it off as an original thought. No need to mention Bok's book, the student thinks, because no one will bother to check, and even if the instructor should happen to recognize this passage, why, the student can plead "forgetting" to give Bok full credit. The student submits an essay containing the following passage incorporated into the narrative text:

> Deceit and violence are two forms of deliberate assault on human beings. Both can coerce people into acting against their will. Most harm that can happen to people through violence can also happen to them through deceit. However, deceit controls more subtly, because it works on belief as well as action. Even Othello, whom few would have dared to try to subdue by force, could be brought to destroy himself and Desdemona through falsehood.

Although it might sound like an A paper to the student, the passage when seen in the context of the rest of the paper may stick out like a sore thumb, and instructors are sensitive to inconsistencies like these. If the student is caught, the results will be an F in the course. Even if not caught red-handed, the student must nevertheless live with the knowledge of this deceit and worry that the dishonesty may at some later point come back to haunt him or her.

How might the student have used this work without falling into plagiarism? One answer is simply to put quotes around the material the student wants to copy verbatim—and then give a complete citation. Another option is to paraphrase the work and to give full credit to the original author. In sum, if someone else has said something much better than you can ever hope to say it, quote (and cite) or paraphrase (and cite) the other source. Here is a proper paraphrase, requiring minimal effort, to be incorporated in the narrative text of the student's paper:

> Bok (1978) makes the case that deceit and violence "can coerce people into acting against their will" (p. 18). Deceit, she argues, controls more subtly because it affects belief. Using a literary analogy, Bok observes, "Even Othello, whom few would have dared to try to subdue by force, could be brought to destroy himself and Desdemona through falsehood" (p. 18).

Electronic plagiarizing is no more acceptable than plagiarizing from printed matter. If you find something on the Internet you want to use, the same considerations of honesty apply. Some instructors have told us how they randomly check students' titles and phraseology using a specialized search engine to look for stolen material or uncredited citations. One instructor told us how he typed the title of a student's paper into a search engine and the entire paper came up on a Web site! With the growing accessibility of specialized search tools engineered to detect this problem, the likelihood of not getting caught is diminishing rapidly. As previously mentioned, it is a good idea to keep your notes, outlines, and rough drafts, because instructors will ask students for such material if a question arises about the originality of their work.

Lazy Writing

On hearing that quotations and citations are not construed by definition as plagiarism, some lazy students submit papers saturated with quoted material. Unless you feel it is absolutely essential, avoid quoting lengthy passages throughout a paper. What, then, would be appropriate occasions for quoting someone? One situation would be if you were describing two competing views and wanted to ensure representing both positions fairly. Another situation is when someone's language is so expressive and convincing that you believe it would improve your presentation to quote a portion of it.

Thus, there are occasions when it may be advisable to quote something (with a citation, of course). However, quoting a statement that is not particularly momentous or poignant signals lazy writing. Your instructor expects your paper to reflect *your* thoughts after you have examined and synthesized material from sources you found pertinent. The penalty for lazy writing is not as severe as that for plagiarism, but it may mean a reduced grade in writing-intensive courses.

The reason for a lowered grade is that lazy writing conveys the impression that the student has not put very much effort into the assignment. Furthermore, if you really cannot say it in your own words, your instructor will conclude that you do not understand it well enough to write about it.

Tone

As you write, there are certain basic style points to keep in mind. The *tone* of your paper is the manner and attitude that are reflected in the way you express your ideas. Your writing should not sound arrogant or pompous, nor should it be either dull or flowery. How can you create an appropriate tone in a scholarly essay or research report in psychology? The answer is that it takes a lot of practice, and in the process of becoming skilled, you can learn by paying attention to how successful researchers and scholars express their ideas in an appropriate tone.

Here are some tips on how to create the right tone:

- ◆ Strive for an explicit, straightforward, interesting but not emotional way of expressing your thoughts, findings, and conclusions (as illustrated in the sample papers).
- ◆ Try not to sound stilted or uncomfortably formal (Instead of saying, "In the opinion of this writer . . .", just state your opinion—period).
- ◆ Don't write in such a casual or informal way, however, that your paper reads like a letter to a favorite aunt ("Here's what Jones and Smith say . . ." or "So I told the research participants . . .").
- ◆ Try not to sound slick, like the glib reports on network TV and in supermarket tabloids.
- ◆ Strive for an objective, direct tone that keeps your reader subordinate to the material you are presenting. Instead of saying, "The reader will note that the results were . . . ," say, "The results were . . ."
- ◆ If your instructor finds it acceptable, don't be afraid to use the first person, but don't refer to yourself as *we* unless you are clearly referring to a collaborative effort with someone else.
- ◆ Avoid wordiness. A famous writing manual is *The Elements of Style* (Allyn & Bacon, 2000) by William Strunk, Jr., and E. B. White. One of Professor Strunk's admonitions is "Omit needless words. Omit needless words. Omit needless words."

Nonsexist Language

The question of *word gender* has become a matter of some sensitivity among many writers. One reason to discourage sex bias in written and spoken communication is that words can influence people's thoughts and deeds, and we do not want to reinforce stereotypes or prejudiced behaviors. However, there is sometimes a good reason not to use gender-free pronouns. Suppose a new drug has been tested only on male participants. If the researchers used only gender-free pronouns when referring to their participants, a reader might mistakenly infer that the results apply to both sexes.

The point, of course, is to think before you write. In her book *The Elements of Nonsexist Usage* (Prentice Hall, 1990), Val Dumond made the following observation concerning overuse of the word *man:* "When the word is used, that is the mental picture that is formed. The picture is what simultaneously represents a conceptual meaning to the interpreter. Since a female picture does not come to mind when the word *man* is used, it would follow that man does not represent in any way a female human" (p. 1).

When the issues of nonsexist language first gained prominence, writers used contrived words such as *s/he* and *he/she* to avoid sexist language. Experienced writers and editors have discovered various ways to circumvent the awkwardness of such forms and also the possible trap of gender-biased language. In general, beware of masculine nouns and pronouns that will give a sex bias to your writing. There are two simple rules:

◆ Use plural pronouns when you are referring to both genders—for instance, "They did . . ." instead of "He did . . ." and ". . . to them" instead of ". . . to him."
◆ Use masculine and feminine pronouns if the situation calls for them. For example, if the study you are discussing used only male research participants, the masculine pronouns are accurate. The forms *he/she* and *s/he* not only are awkward but in this case would mislead the reader into thinking that the research participants were both women and men.

Voice

The verb forms you use in your writing can speak with one of two voices: active or passive. You write in the *active voice* when you represent the subject of your sentence as performing the action expressed by your verb ("The study participant responded by . . ."). You write in the *passive voice* when the subject of your sentence undergoes the action expressed by your verb ("The response was made by the study participant . . .").

If you try to rely mainly on the active voice, you will have a more vital, compelling style:

Active Voice (Good)

Eleanor Gibson (1988) argued that perceptual development in humans is "an ever-spiraling path of discovery" (p. 37).

Passive Voice (Not as Good)

It was argued by Eleanor Gibson (1988) that perceptual development in humans is "an ever-spiraling path of discovery" (p. 37).

This quoted passage also illustrates when it is advisable to quote. The reason the student chose this fragment is that it is especially expressive and eloquent, whereas trying to paraphrase it might not capture Gibson's idea with the same articulacy. Furthermore, quoting such an eminent authority as Eleanor Gibson lends weight to the student's development of a particular argument.

Verb Tense

The verb tenses you use in your paper can get into a tangle unless you observe the following basic rules:

◆ Use the *past tense* to report studies that were done in the past ("Jones and Smith found . . ."). If you are writing a research report, both the method and results sections can usually be written in the past tense because your study has already been accomplished ("In this study, data *were* collected . . ." and "In these questionnaires, there *were* . . .").

◆ Use the *present tense* to define terms ("Multiplex, in this context, *means* . . ." and "A stereotype *is* defined as . . ."). The present tense is also frequently used to state a general hypothesis or to make a general claim ("Winter days *are* generally shorter than summer days").

◆ The *future tense* can be saved for the section of your paper in which you discuss implications for further investigation ("Future research *will be* necessary . . ."). But it is not essential to use the future tense. Instead, you could say, "Further investigation *is* warranted. . . ."

Notice that three periods appear at the end of some of the examples in the above list. The name for these periods is an *ellipsis mark*, and its purpose in these examples is to indicate that the sentences continue. Although as a general rule the ellipsis is not used at the end of a quotation, we use it in these examples just to introduce you to this punctuation mark. Typically, the ellipsis is used somewhere in the middle of a lengthy quoted passage to indicate that selected words have been omitted.

Agreement of Subject and Verb

Make sure each sentence expresses a complete thought and has a *subject* (in general terms, something that performs the action) and a *verb* (an action that is performed or a state of being).

Subject and Verb Agree

The study participants [subject] were [verb] introductory psychology students who were fulfilling a course requirement.

Because the subject is plural (*study participants*), the verb form used (*were*) is also plural. Thus, the verb and subject agree, a basic rule of grammar.

In most sentence forms, achieving this agreement is a simple matter. But trouble can sometimes arise, so here are some tips:

◆ When you use *collective nouns* (those that name a group), they can be either singular or plural—for example, *committee, team, faculty.* When you think of the group as a single unit, use a singular verb ("The union *is* ready to settle"). Plurals are called for when you want to refer to the components of a group ("The faculty *were* divided on the issue").

◆ Trouble can pop up when words come between subject and verb: "Therapy [singular subject], in combination with behavioral organic methods of weight gain, exemplifies [singular verb form] this approach." It would be incorrect to write, "Therapy, in combination with behavioral organic methods of weight gain, *exemplify* [plural verb form] this approach."

◆ Use a *singular verb form* after the following: *each, either, everyone, someone, neither, nobody.* Here is a correct usage: "When everyone is ready, the experiment will begin."

Common Usage Errors

Confusing Homonyms

Instructors see frequent usage errors in student papers. The inside front cover of this manual lists pairs of words that are both pronounced similarly (*homonyms*) and often confused with one another, such as *accept* ("receive") and *except* ("other than").

Another pair of confusing homonyms is *affect* and *effect.* Here are some tips to help you sort them out:

◆ In their most common form, *effect* is a noun meaning "outcome" (as in "Aggression is often an *effect* of frustration"), whereas *affect* is a verb meaning "to influence" (as in "Frustration *affects* how a person behaves").

◆ However, *effect* can also be used as a verb meaning "to bring about" (as in "The clinical intervention *effected* a measurable improvement").

◆ And *affect* can also be used as a noun meaning "emotion" (as in "Several of the patients participating in this clinical trial exhibited positive *affect*").

Incorrect Use of Singular and Plural

Another potential source of problems is the incorrect use of the singular and plural of some familiar terms, for instance:

Singular	*Plural*
analysis	analyses
anomaly	anomalies
appendix	appendixes or appendices (both are correct)
criterion	criteria
datum	data
hypothesis	hypotheses
phenomenon	phenomena
stimulus	stimuli

For example, one common usage error is the confusion of *phenomena* [plural term] with *phenomenon* [singular term]. It would be incorrect to write, "This [singular pronoun] phenomena [plural subject] is [singular verb] of interest." The correct form is either "This phenomenon is . . ." or "These phenomena are . . ."

Although you will find that words like *data* and *media* are often construed as singular, the general rule is that until there is no question about something's being correct, it is good to be on the safe side (so as not to be criticized by sticklers). In this case, the safe side is to interpret *data* and *media* as plural words. Thus, it would be unsafe to write, "The data [plural subject] indicates [singular verb] . . ." or "The data shows . . ." To be on the safe side, you would write, "The data indicate . . ." or "The data show . . ."

Between and Among

Another common source of confusion is in the misuse of the words *between* and *among*. As a general rule, use *between* when you are referring to two items only; use *among* when there are more than two items. For example, it would be incorrect to write "between the three of them."

There is, however, one anomaly that you can do nothing about correcting. In the analysis of variance (abbreviated ANOVA), conventional usage says "between sum of squares" and the "between mean square," even if the number of conditions being compared is more than two.

Prefixes

Other common problems concern the use of some *prefixes* in psychological terms:

- The prefix *inter-* means "between" (for example, *interpersonal* means "between persons"); the prefix *intra-* means "within" (for example, *intrapersonal* means "within the person").
- The prefix *intro-* means "inward" or "within"; the prefix *extra-* means "outside" or "beyond." The psychological term *introverted* thus refers to an "inner-directed personality"; the term *extraverted* indicates an "outer-directed personality."

◆ The prefix *hyper-* means "too much"; the prefix *hypo-* means "too little." Hence, the term *hypothyroidism* refers to a deficiency of thyroid hormone. *Hyperthyroidism* denotes an excess of thyroid hormone, and a *hyperactive* child is one who is excessively active.

Participants Versus Subjects

Although not strictly a usage error, referring to human beings who participated in a study as *subjects* is no longer recommended by the APA. Although the term commonly appears in other than APA publications, the reasoning of those who object is that "subjects" sounds passive and nondescriptive, whereas human beings are active agents who initiate as well as react. The APA recommends that writers use *participants* as a general term instead of *subjects*, but that writers also try to be more specific by using terms such as *respondents*, *children*, *patients*, *clients*—with the particular choice of a term depending on the nature or role of those persons who participated in the study.

Numerals

Another source of bafflement can be the proper use of numerals in the APA style. In general, the APA recommends spelling out single-digit figures (one, two, three, four, five, six, seven, eight, nine) and using figures (10, 20, 30, 40) for numbers with more than one digit. However, there are exceptions to this rule. Here are some guidelines to help you decide when to spell out numbers and when to use figures for numbers:

◆ Although it is recommended that you not begin a sentence with a number, if you must do so, then spell it out ("Twenty-nine students volunteered for this study" or "Fourteen percent of all the participants responded in the affirmative").
◆ Numbers expressed as words in phrases and sentences should be spelled out (as in "two-tailed test" or the sentence "Only two of the participants refused to go further in the study").
◆ Spell out *zero* and *one* when they are easier to understand than *0* and *1* ("zero-sum game" or "one-word response").
◆ When single-digit numbers are part of a numerical group, use figures (for example, in the sample essay in Appendix A, John Smith states that Robert Sternberg was "1 of 11 coauthors of the APA report by Neisser et al."; another example would be "5 of the 25 participants failed to answer this question").
◆ Use figures for all numbers—even one-digit numbers—that immediately precede a unit of measurement (for example, 3 cm or 9 mg).
◆ Use figures for units of age and time (4-year-old, 3 months, 2 days, 9 minutes), units of measurement (1 million, 3%), and numbers used in reference lists (pp. 4–6, 2nd ed., Vol. 4).

◆ Use whatever is the universally accepted style for well-known expressions (the Ten Commandments).

Other APA rules for reporting singular and plural numbers, long sequences of numbers, and physical measurements are the following:

◆ When reporting the plurals of numbers, add an *s* without an apostrophe. So the plural of 1990 would be 1990s, and the plural of 20 would be 20s.
◆ Commas are used between groups of three digits, except for page numbers (page 1225), binary digits (001001), serial numbers (345789), degrees of freedom, and numbers to the right of a decimal point (2,300.1357).
◆ When reporting physical units, use the metric system. For example, 1 foot is reported as .3048 m (or meter, with no period after the *m*), and 1 inch becomes .0254 m.

More on Punctuation

Periods

Besides the proper use of commas in reporting numbers, there are various other rules for the use of punctuation marks in your writing. Notice above that there was no period after the *m* symbol for meter, because the APA style is not to use a period after a symbol, except when the symbol is at the end of a sentence (a *period* always ends a declarative sentence). Periods are, however, used following an abbreviation other than a physical unit, as in the following common abbreviations of Latin words:

cf.	from *confer* ("compare")
e.g.	from *exempli gratia* ("for example")
et al.	from *et alia* ("and others")
et seq.	from *et sequens* ("and following")
ibid.	from *ibidem* ("in the same place")
i.e.	from *id est* ("that is")
op. cit.	from *opere citato* ("in the work cited")
viz.	from *videlicet* ("namely")

If you continually write *eg.* or *et. al.* in your paper, you will be telling the instructor, "I don't know the meaning of these terms!" The reason, of course, is that *e.g.* is the abbreviation of two words, not one. Writing *eg.* announces that you believe (mistakenly) it is the abbreviation of one word. Putting a period after *et* tells the instructor that you believe (again, mistakenly) it is an abbreviation, which it is not; it is an entire Latin word.

With the exception of *et al.*, if you use any of these Latin abbreviations, the APA manual requires that they be used only in parentheses and tabular material, and that these abbreviations otherwise be spelled out. As an illustration, take the expression "for example," which you would write as "e.g." and place in parentheses, as in the following:

Herrnstein and Murray's (1994) book was widely debated (e.g., Andery & Serio, 1997; Andrews & Nelkin, 1996; Carroll, 1997).

Not used in parentheses, it is spelled out rather than abbreviated:

Herrnstein and Murray's (1994) book was widely debated; see, for example, work by Andery and Serio (1997), Andrews and Nelkin (1996), and Carroll (1997).

The abbreviation *et al.*, however, when used in reference lists and in text, does not have to be in parentheses.

Other abbreviations that are followed by a period are the short forms of English words:

anon.	for *anonymous*
ch.	for *chapter*
diagr.	for *diagram*
ed.	for *editor* or *edition*
fig.	for *figure*
ms.	for *manuscript*
p.	for *page*
pp.	for *pages*
rev.	for *revised*
v.	for *versus* (in references and text citations of court cases)
vol.	for *volume*
vs.	for *versus, against*

Another important point is that, except for common abbreviations like those above, most abbreviations for terms are first spelled out for the reader. Thus, in the sample essay, John Smith writes, ". . . the psychometric idea of a general trait (*g*)," which tells the reader that the abbreviation *g* is defined as a general trait. If you wanted to refer repeatedly to the term *reaction time* or to an instrument called the Humboldt Upside-Down Test, you would write "reaction time (RT)" or the "Humboldt Upside-Down Test (HUDT)" the first time you mentioned the term and then use the abbreviation RT or HUDT whenever you referred to the same term again.

The APA's exception to this rule is that abbreviations that you can find listed as word entries in *Webster's Collegiate Dictionary* do not need to be defined first. For example, the abbreviations IQ, REM, AIDS, HIV, and ESP appear as words in *Webster's* and thus do not need to be defined or set off in parentheses the first time they are used in a psychology paper.

Commas and Semicolons

We mentioned when commas are used and not used in numbers. Some other uses of the *comma* include the following:

- ◆ Use commas to separate each of three or more items in a series ("Smith, Jones, and Brown" or "high, medium, and low scorers").
- ◆ Use commas to set off introductory phrases in a sentence ("In another experiment performed 10 years later, the same researchers found . . .").
- ◆ Use commas to set off thoughts or phrases that are incidental to, or that qualify, the basic idea of the sentence ("This variable, although not part of the researchers' main hypothesis, was also examined").
- ◆ Put a comma before coordinating conjunctions (*and, but, or, nor, yet*) when they join independent clauses ("The subject lost weight, but he was still able to . . .").
- ◆ Put a comma between adjectives that could conceivably be joined with the word *and* (called *coordinate adjectives*), such as "The quick, brown fox jumped. . . ."

A common error is to insert a comma before a transitional expression such as *however, moreover,* or *therefore* when it is used to connect two complete clauses in a compound sentence. For example, "The participants voiced no concerns, however, it was quite obvious that they were uncomfortable" clearly consists of two complete clauses. Instead of a comma before *however,* a *semicolon* (;) should be used. Alternatively, this compound sentence can easily be divided into two sentences: "The participants voiced no concerns. However, it was quite obvious that they were uncomfortable." Still another alternative is to replace the transitional expression *however* with the conjunction *but* preceded by a comma: "The participants voiced no concerns, but it was quite obvious that they were uncomfortable."

As a general rule, a semicolon is called for when the thoughts in the two independent clauses are close, and the writer wishes to emphasize this point or to contrast the two thoughts. The following is an example of the appropriate use of a semicolon for connecting thoughts:

> Anorexia nervosa is a disorder in which the victims literally starve themselves; despite their emaciated appearance, they consider themselves overweight.

In most instances, however, these long sentences can be divided into shorter ones, which will be clearer:

> Anorexia nervosa is a disorder in which the victims literally starve themselves. Despite their emaciated appearance, they consider themselves overweight.

The Colon

Generally, the *colon* (:) is used to indicate that a list will follow, or to introduce an amplification. The colon tells the reader, "Note what follows."

Here is an example in which we see a colon used to indicate that a list follows:

Subjects were given the following items: (a) four calling birds, (b) three French hens, (c) two turtle doves . . .

An example of the amplification use of a colon is the title of Jane Doe's research report. Another example of amplification would be

Gardner (1983) postulated two forms of the personal intelligences: interpersonal and intrapersonal intelligence.

For another use of the colon, observe in the reference lists of the two sample papers at the end of this book that a colon is inserted between the place of publication of a book and the name of the publisher—for example, "Belmont, CA: Wadsworth" or "Boston: McGraw-Hill" or "Upper Saddle River, NJ: Prentice Hall" or "Mahwah, NJ: Erlbaum." We will have more to say about the punctuation used in references in the next chapter.

Punctuation in Quoted Passages

Previously, we mentioned the ellipsis mark (. . .) used in quoted passages to indicate that selected words have been intentionally omitted. You will sometimes also see in quoted passages brackets ([ ]) with words inside. The use of brackets tells us that the words are not part of the original quotation but were inserted by the writer who is using this quoted material. For example, omitting some words might make a quoted passage seem grammatically incorrect or might make something unclear, but either of these problems can be easily fixed by the insertion of a few connecting words in brackets.

Earlier, we also mentioned the importance of putting quotation marks around words that are quoted. An exception is when a quotation is 40 or more words, in which case it is set off from the body of the text by means of indented margins, and quotation marks are omitted. However, if there is an internal quotation within the longer quotation, then *double quotation marks* (". . .") are inserted around the quote within a quote, as in the following example:

What practical implications did Rosenthal and Jacobson (1968) draw from their research findings? They wrote:

As teacher-training institutions begin to teach the possibility that teachers' expectations of their pupils' performance may serve as self-fulfilling prophecies, there may be a new expectancy created. The new expectancy may be that children can learn more than had been believed possible, an expectation held by many educational theorists, though for quite different reasons. . . . The new expectancy, at the very least, will make it more difficult when they encounter the educationally disadvantaged for teachers to think, "Well, after all, what can you expect?" The man [*sic*] on the street may be permitted his opinions and prophecies of the unkempt children loitering in a dreary schoolyard. The teacher in the schoolroom may need to learn that those same prophecies within her [*sic*] may be fulfilled; she is no casual passer-by. Perhaps Pygmalion in the classroom is more her role. (pp. 181–182)

When a quoted passage is fewer than 40 words, double quotation marks are used and the passage is simply inserted in the text as part of the narrative. If there is a smaller quote within the quoted passage, then *single quotation marks* ('. . .') are used to set off the quote within a quote, as in the following sentence:

Participant B responded, "My feeling about this difficult situation was summed up in a nutshell by Jim when he said, 'It's a tough job, but somebody has to do it.'"

As this example also illustrates, if the appropriate punctuation is a period (as shown at the end of this sentence), it is included *within* the quotation marks. The same rule applies to a comma; it is inserted within the quotation marks. But if the appropriate punctuation is a colon or a semicolon, it is inserted *after* the closing quotation marks.

In the lengthy quote above, which begins, "As teacher-training institutions . . ." and ends ". . . in the classroom is more her role," notice that the numbers of the pages on which the passage appears in Rosenthal and Jacobson's book are shown in parentheses at the end. Notice also that the word *sic* (Latin, meaning "thus") is inserted in brackets in two places; it indicates that a word or phrase that appears strange or incorrect is quoted verbatim. Thus, if you wanted to make the point that a quoted passage ignores gender, you insert in brackets the word *sic* as shown. But observe that we did not insert *sic* after every gender term. In the first sentence, the masculine pronoun *his* was not set off by *sic* because the reference is "man on the street." In the second sentence, the feminine pronoun *she* is also not set off, because the referent is "within her."

Revising

In the next chapter, we consider the details of producing your final draft. Revising the first draft of your paper is best done after you have been able to leave the manuscript entirely. When you approach your writing after having taken such a break (ideally, 24 hours or more), your critical powers will be sharper. Syntax errors, lapses in logic, and other problems will become evident, so that smoothing out these sections will be a relatively simple chore.

As you reread and polish your writing, consider the following suggestions:

- ◆ Be concise.
- ◆ Break up long paragraphs that contain a lot of disparate ideas into smaller, more coherent paragraphs.
- ◆ Be specific.

- Choose words for what they mean, not just for how they sound.
- Double-check punctuation.
- Don't use a long word when a short word will do.
- Don't be redundant (for example, "most unique" is redundant).
- Don't let spelling errors mar your writing.
- If you are unsure about how to spell a word, use the spell check function on your word processor; if the answer you get seems ambiguous, check your dictionary.

If you are new to word processing (or are learning a new word-processing program), be sure you know how to save and back up your work when you are ready to start composing and revising. A good system will do this for you automatically at regular intervals, but you must specify the interval you want. You never know when the electricity will suddenly go out or someone will playfully or accidentally hit a wrong key, or you yourself might be distracted and hit a wrong key and send your latest work into oblivion.

Making a backup means not only storing something inside the computer's hard drive (that is, if it's *your* PC) but also copying it onto a floppy disk or a ZIP disk. Our habit is also to make a printout every few days. Having a printed copy will allow you to inspect and modify the layout to make sure it looks the way you want it to. It also allows you to polish your writing in a format that is tangible. Sometimes spelling errors and murky passages that are less apparent on-screen jump out as your eye traverses a printed page.

7

PRODUCING THE
FINAL DRAFT

This chapter provides you with guidelines and tips for producing a finished product. The layout and production of your final draft are like the icing on a cake. If the underlying structure is sound, the result will be smooth and predictable.

General Pointers

Working with a word processor means that the steps involved in first drafts, revisions, and final drafts are telescoped. These stages lose their formal definition because the computer allows you, with the stroke of a key or the click of a mouse, to shift or change words, sentences, paragraphs, and even entire sections as you compose and revise. In the old days, when students could use only a typewriter, it was painfully difficult to revise, because they had to equip themselves with scissors and glue to literally cut and paste and then each time had to retype those sections of the paper that had been changed. Notes, long quotations, references, tables, and figures that you will need for your final draft can be stored in your computer's memory or on a disk and can be retrieved as needed. The computer is not a substitute for the hard work of organizing your ideas, thinking them through, and expressing them clearly, but it releases you from an enormous amount of drudgery.

Word-processing systems have spell checkers and grammar checkers, which are designed to flag mistakes, offer alternatives, and let you choose whether to make a particular change or to ignore all of the alternative recommendations. These programs are not infallible, so do not let them lull you into a false sense of security or into thinking that they are a substitute for careful proofreading of your final manuscript. Your spell checker is based on a dictionary (actually a word inventory) in the word-processing system, but it is possible that many technical terms that psychologists and other professionals use may not be present in your word-processing inventory. If your spell checker flags a word that you know is spelled correctly, simply add the correct spelling to the word inventory. Notice that there are lists of commonly misspelled words in the front and back covers of this manual; if you peruse this list once you have written a first draft of your proposal or final paper, some words may stand out as possible mistakes in your paper that the spell checker missed.

Grammar checkers are designed to flag a sentence that violates a particular grammar or style rule. When it encounters what it has been programmed to define as a problem, a grammar dialog box appears on the screen, and you are asked whether you want to accept a suggestion or ignore it. You can set up the word processor so that the grammar checker automatically searches for violations as you write and flags them as they are encountered, or you can simply turn off the grammar checker and use it only when you want it. As many experienced writers know, grammar checkers can be maddening because they often "catch" acceptable stylistic variations and fail to recognize stylistic requirements that may have been violated. Although it is essential to keep the spell checker active, many writers prefer not to use the grammar checker and instead depend on their own eyes and experience to catch mistakes and correct them.

Another tool on your word processor that can be very useful is the thesaurus, which you access by clicking on the appropriate menu option (or right-clicking in Word 98 or later versions, and then opening on the Synonyms submenu). In Chapter Two, we mentioned the thesaurus that PsycINFO has for identifying search-word synonyms. The thesaurus on your word processor looks up synonyms for words or phrases, and you then choose whether to replace a word with one of the synonyms. However, you need to make sure that the replacement word means the same thing as your original word, which only you can decide. If you are not absolutely sure, look up the replacement word in your dictionary.

Here are more general pointers as you set about producing the final product:

◆ Make sure the type is legible. If it is faint, invest in a new cartridge.
◆ Use double line spacing, and print on only one side of the sheet of paper, inserting a page header in the upper right corner and numbering pages as the two sample papers illustrate.
◆ Make a second copy of the finished paper. The original is for your instructor, and the duplicate copy will ensure the immediate availability of an exact spare copy in case of an unforeseen problem.
◆ Don't format your word processor to create a justified (even) right margin, which produces a block effect and, sometimes, odd spacing within lines. Instead, let the right margin remain ragged (uneven), as the APA manual stipulates.
◆ Use a 12-point typeface, preferably Times New Roman or Courier, both of which are known as *serif* typefaces, so called because of the

tiny line that finishes off a main stroke of a letter. If you are lettering drawings and figures, however, use a typeface without a serif (called *sans serif typefaces*) because it provides a sharper visual presentation in graphics.

◆ Don't use the letter *l* to represent the numeral one or the letter *o* to represent a zero; instead use the separate 1 and 0 keys for these digits. Also, don't use *X* to represent chi; instead, insert the proper symbol (χ) using the appropriate submenu, or else write it in by hand.

◆ The style recommended by the APA for manuscripts submitted for publication is to use one space following all punctuation, including the space between the end and beginning of sentences. However, if you are in the habit of inserting two spaces after a period (which we are), do what is comfortable. (The APA also does not reject manuscripts on the basis of the spacing around punctuation.)

We turn now to other specifics of layout and processing that will help to give your finished paper a pleasing appearance.

Title Page Format

Glance at the title pages of the two sample papers at the end of this book. The title summarizes the main idea of the project and is centered on the page. (Notice that the title appears again on page 3 of each sample paper.) A good title is succinct and yet adequately describes to the reader the gist of the work. You will already have arrived at a working title when narrowing your topic and drafting a proposal (Chapter Three). That title can now be changed or made more specific if you feel it is no longer accurate or completely descriptive of the finished product. (Incidentally, the APA style is to capitalize prepositions of four or more letters in titles and headings, so you would capitalize *With* or *From* if it appears in the title of your paper.)

Other information is also shown on the title page of these sample papers:

The page header and page number
The student's name (called the *byline*)
The number and name of the course or sequence for which the paper was
    written
The instructor's or adviser's name
The date the paper will be submitted

As noted in Chapter Six, the page number in the upper-right corner is accompanied (on every page) by one or more words. These words are called *page headers*, and their purpose is to make it easy for the reader to identify each manuscript page if pages become separated. It is easy enough to insert a page header with most word-processing programs. As you revise—cutting and pasting—the word processor will automatically update the page numbers.

Showing the instructor's name (if the paper is submitted for a course) or the adviser's name (if the paper is submitted to fulfill some other requirement, such as a "prelim" paper) is a courtesy. If the paper is a thesis, another courtesy is to include an acknowledgment page (after the title page) on which you thank your adviser and any others who extended a helping hand as you worked on your project. Incidentally, theses also usually include a table of contents page.

Headings

It is customary to break up the text of a term paper or research report with brief but informative headings. One purpose of these headings is to provide a conceptual map that enables readers to understand exactly where they are as they examine the sequence of topics or issues discussed in the paper. Another purpose is to organize the writer's thinking, so that topics that belong in one section do not accidentally stray into another section where they do not belong. A third purpose is to shepherd readers through the logical flow of the paper, from the most important to the least important (but still relevant) topics, issues, or information.

If you are writing an essay, you should be able to derive these headings from the outline of your essay. Observe, for example, how John Smith's headings and subheadings lend symmetry to his essay, showing its progressive development in concise phrases. John's essay uses two formats of headings: center and flush left. *Center headings* are used to separate the paper into major sections, are written in uppercase and lowercase letters, and are not italicized (or underlined):

Two General Conceptions of Intelligence
Gardner's Theory of Multiple Intelligences
Two Main Criticisms of Multiplex Theories
Conclusions

To subdivide these major sections, John uses *subheadings* that are flush left, in italics, and in uppercase and lowercase. John uses three subheadings to partition the major section labeled "Gardner's Theory of Multiple Intelligences":

Gardner's Notion of Intelligence
Seven Kinds of Intelligence
Independence of Abilities

If he had needed to use a second level of subheadings, they would be indented, italicized, and followed by a period, with the body of the text immediately following the subheading. For example, they might look like the following had he wanted to partition the section labeled *"Seven Kinds of Intelligence"* and begun with a *"Logical-Mathematical"* subheading:

Seven Kinds of Intelligence
　　Logical-Mathematical. One traditional type of intelligence, called "logical-mathematical" by Gardner (1985), refers to . . .

If you are writing a research report, you simply use headings that are inherent in the structure of virtually all research reports in psychology when only a single study or experiment is reported. In Jane Doe's report in Appendix B, under the major heading of "Method," she uses "*Participants*" and "*Procedure*" as subheadings to partition this section. Had she then subdivided these two subsections, she would have used the second-level subheading that we described above (i.e., indented, italicized, and followed by a period, with the text immediately following). There are further levels of subheadings that writers preparing more lengthy or complex manuscripts can use, but the ones illustrated here should suffice for students writing essays and research reports.

Italicizing

Before the days of word processors, underlining was used to indicate to typesetters that selected text was to be set in italics. Nowadays, it is a simple matter to format text in italics; you just click and type, or highlight and click. The APA does not object, however, if authors of manuscripts submitted for publication use underlining rather than italics, because once a paper is accepted for publication, the copyeditor inserts an underline anyway. Conventional usage also calls for the titles of books mentioned in the body of the text to be italicized ("In *Pygmalion in the Classroom,* Rosenthal and Jacobson wrote that . . .").
　　Italicizing is also used in several other ways:

- Letters used as statistical symbols are italicized: *F, N, n, P, p, t, Z,* and so forth. Note that some symbols are in lowercase, and this can be very important. For example, an uppercase *N* indicates the total number of sampling units, but a lowercase *n* indicates the number of units in a subsample of *N*.
- However, Greek letters used as statistical symbols are not italicized—for example, the symbol for chi-square (χ^2), the symbol instructing us to sum a set of scores (Σ), the symbol for the standard deviation of a population of scores (σ), and the symbol for the variance of a population of scores (σ^2).
- In reference lists, volume numbers of journal articles and titles of books and journals are italicized.
- Words that you wish to emphasize are italicized, but this device should be used sparingly ("Effective teaching, the authors asserted, will come only from the teachers' firm belief that their pupils *can* perform.").
- Words used to illustrate are also italicized ("the term *knowing* . . ." or ". . . is called *knowing*"). For example, John Smith writes, "People use

the word *intelligence* and its various synonyms . . ." and "The second major view . . . is characterized here as the *multiplex view* because . . .").

In the rare event that a student wants to insert into a paper a statistical formula with superscripts and subscripts, it can be a real problem to selectively italicize parts of the formula. One option is to use the equation editor function and let it go at that, and another option is to write the equation by hand. If you are using a program such as *MathType,* it gives you the option of whether to use italics or not for each unit of an equation. If you are inserting statistical formulas into the appendix of your research report, you can simply write them out by hand as illustrated in Jane's report.

Citations in Text

There are several simple conventions for citing an author's work in the narrative text of a paper. The purpose of a citation is to make it easy for the reader to identify the source of a quotation or an idea and then to locate the particular reference in the list at the end of the paper. The author-date method is the format stipulated in the APA manual. The surname of the author and the year of publication are inserted in the text at the appropriate point.

Here are two general rules and the exceptions:

◆ Do not list any publication in your reference list that you do not cite. The exception to this rule would be if you were developing an extensive bibliography of references and wanted to list every relevant article and book on the subject, whether you discussed them in your manuscript or not. Of course, you would not be expected to compile such a bibliography for an essay or a research report in a course.

◆ Do not cite any source material in the text without placing it in the reference list. The exception to this rule would be a personal communication cited in the text, because it is unnecessary to put it in the list of references as well.

If you want to cite a source that you did not read yourself, make it clear that you are borrowing someone else's citation (called a *secondary citation*). But use a secondary source only if the original source is unavailable to you; otherwise examine and cite the original source yourself. The reason to refrain from using secondary sources is that there is no guarantee that the material you want to cite is described correctly in the secondary source.

If you must use a secondary source for information that you did not read in the original form, here is the way to cite it in the text:

Citation of Secondary Source

In Virgil's epic poem, *The Aeneid* (as cited in Allport and Postman, 1947), the following characterization of rumor appears: . . .

In general, there are two categories of citations in students' research reports and essays: citations that appear as part of the narrative text and citations inserted in alphabetical order (and then by year if the same author is cited twice) entirely in parentheses within the text. Notice in the first example below that the word *and* is spelled out in a narrative citation, whereas, in the second example, an ampersand (&) is used in a parenthetical citation:

Citation Appearing as Part of Text

Baldwin, Doyle, Kern, Mithalal, and Stella (1991) asked a sample of child-care providers to describe incidents in which . . .

Citation Entirely in Parentheses

Institutional review boards may harbor quite different biases regarding the ethical risks of the studies they are asked to evaluate (e.g., Ceci, Peters, & Plotkin, 1985; Hamsher & Reznikoff, 1967; Kallgren & Kenrick, 1990; Schlenker & Forsyth, 1977).

These examples also illustrate the convention of author-date citations that dictates the listing of the surnames of up to five authors the first time the citation is given. In subsequent citations, if there are more than two authors, you give the surname of only the first author, followed by "et al." and the date ("Baldwin et al."). Here are two further examples:

Subsequent Citation as Part of Text

Ceci et al. (1985) found that one research proposal, approved without changes in one institution, was amended at another institution in the same city.

Subsequent Citation Entirely in Parentheses

One research proposal, approved without changes in one institution, was amended at another institution in the same city (Ceci et al., 1985).

To cite an e-mail message or a written communication you have received, you would refer to it as a personal communication, but (as previously mentioned) you would not list it again in your references section:

Personal Communication as Part of Text

An alternative approach, noted by T. E. Schoenfelder (personal communication, August 12, 2001), would explain investment decisions within the framework of behavioral decision theory.

Personal Communication in Parentheses

An alternative approach would explain investment decisions within the framework of behavioral decision theory (T. E. Schoenfelder, personal communication, August 12, 2001).

To cite a specific document obtained from a Web site, you would use a format similar to that for printed material (as shown above). If all you want is to cite a particular Web site but not a specific document from a Web site, you would give the address of the site but not include it in your References section:

Web Site Citation

Information about the *Publication Manual of the American Psychological Association* (5th ed.) can be found on the *APA Publication Manual* Web site (http://www.apastyle.org).

Here are some other specific rules that cover most of the cases that students encounter:

♦ If you are citing a series of works, the proper sequence is by alphabetical order of the surname of the first author and then by chronological order (Brecher, 1999; DiClemente, 2000; DiFonzo & Bordia, 1993; Frei, 2002; Freeman, 1999; Gergen & Shotter, 1985, 1988; Stern, in press; Strohmetz, 1997; Trimble, in press; Wells & Lafleur, 1997).
♦ Two or more works published by the same author in the same year are designated as *a*, *b*, *c*, and so on (Hantula, 2001a, 2001b, 2001c). In the references section, the alphabetical order of the works' titles determines the sequence when there is more than one work by the author in the same year.
♦ Work accepted for publication but not yet printed is designated "in press" (Aditya, in press); in a list of citations, the rule is to place this work last: (Aditya, 2000, 2001, in press).

What should you do if you run into a problem that these rules do not address? You might check out the APA Web site. However, even the APA seems quite flexible, and does not return manuscripts simply because the format of one unusual citation deviates from the norm. Once the manuscript is accepted for publication, corrections are made during the copyediting process. Thus, keep one general idea in mind as you go beyond these specific guidelines: If you run into a problem, ask yourself whether you could identify a reference based on the citation you have provided. In other words, put yourself in your reader's shoes, but also try to be consistent.

Tables and Figures

Tables and figures can be used to augment the presentation of the results. Often, however, when students include tables in their research reports, they are merely presenting their raw data in a neat format. Save your raw data for the appendix of your report (if your raw data are required), as shown in Jane Doe's report. Keep in mind that statistical tables in results sections of research reports are intended for *summaries* of the raw data rather than for the actual data (see Jane's Table 1) and for other summary results (see Jane's Table 2, which summarizes her ANOVA and linear contrast results).

The APA requires that tables and figures, numbered in the order in which they are first mentioned in the paper, be put on separate pages at the end of the paper (in the case of student papers, the "end of the paper" is defined as the section after the list of references but before the appendix). Observe that the titles of tables in Jane's report are shown above the tables. If these were figures instead of tables, then the title (called the *caption*) would be shown below the figure in the printed article, and the word *Figure* and the number of the figure would be in italics. However, when a paper is submitted for publication, even the figure captions are placed on a separate page, apart from the figures themselves.

These requirements can get confusing for students who are simply writing research reports for a course. To simplify this situation, simply insert the caption below the figure. For example, had Jane used a figure showing a bar diagram (or histogram) instead of a table, the caption below the figure might look like this:

Figure 1. A bar diagram showing the mean tip percentages in four treatment conditions. The standard deviations in these four conditions were 1.46, 1.71, 2.45, and 2.43, respectively, and the sample size was 20 per condition.

As you can see, there is a lot of information crammed into this caption. All this information was neatly condensed in Jane's Table 1, which also lists the mean tip percentages to two decimal places (making it easy for a curious reader to recalculate her test statistics).

If you are using tables, notice that Jane's table titles, in uppercase and lowercase letters, are flush left and italicized. Each column of a table is expected to have a heading, including the left-most column (called the *stub column*, it usually lists the major independent variables). Column headings identify the items below them, and some tables use a hierarchy of headings (also known as *decked heads*) to avoid repeating words. When the top heading in the hierarchy spans the body of the table, it is called a *table spanner*. But these are technical details. Just remember to keep your table headings clear, concise, and informative, so the reader can easily understand what is in the table.

If you are still confused about the difference between a table and a figure, think of figures as bar charts and frequency polygons. Graphics that are photographed or imported from artwork are also considered figures. Because figures sometimes introduce distortions that detract from a clear, concise summary of the data, most researchers prefer to use tables, particularly when giving summary details (group means and standard deviations, for example).

If you must use a figure, be sure not to overcomplicate it. The basic rule is to use only figures that add to the text and not to repeat what you can say very clearly in words. The art of graphic design has been studied by psychologists; if you would like to learn more on this subject, start with Stephen M. Kosslyn's *Elements of Graph Design* (W. H. Freeman, 1994) and Howard Wainer's *Visual Revelations: Graphical Tales of Fate and Deception from Napoleon Bonaparte to Ross Perot* (Erlbaum, 1997).

If you need to add some clarifying or explanatory information to a table, it is customary to place this information below the table, as illustrated in Jane Doe's report. The word *Note* is in italics with a period, and the information follows. To add only a few specific notes to a table, the convention is to use superscript lowercase letters ([a] [b] [c]) or asterisks ([*] [**] [***]). The following cases illustrate this usage:

Superscript Notation

[a]$n = 50$ [b]$n = 62$

Asterisk Notation

[*]$p < .05$ [**]$p < .01$ [***]$p < .0005$

The following guidelines will prove helpful if you decide to use a figure (a bar chart or frequency polygon, for example) instead of a table:

- The figure should be neat, clearly presented, and precisely labeled to augment your discussion.
- The figure should be large enough to read easily.
- The units should progress from small to large.
- The data should be precisely plotted. If you are drawing a figure by hand, use graph paper to help you keep the rows and columns evenly spaced, and then reduce and paste the figure into your report.
- When graphing the relationship between an independent and a dependent variable (or between a predictor variable and a criterion or outcome variable), it is customary to put the independent (or predictor) variable on the horizontal axis (called the x-axis, or the abscissa) and the dependent (or criterion) variable on the vertical axis (the y-axis, or ordinate).

List of References

The list of references starts on a new page, with the title "References" centered on the top of the page. The references are arranged alphabetically by the surname of the author(s) and then by the date of publication. Prefixes (von, Mc, Mac, de, du, for example) can give students pause as they try to figure out how to alphabetize them, and the APA manual has specific rules based on whether or not the prefix is customarily used when the person is referred to. Rather than wrestle with these nuances, simply alphabetize by the article or preposition when you add such names to your list of references.

The standard style rules of the APA manual are to:

◆ Invert all authors' names (that is, last name, first initial, middle initial).
◆ List authors' names in the exact order in which they appear on the title page of the publication.
◆ Use commas to separate authors and an ampersand (&) before the last author.
◆ Give the year the work was copyrighted (the year and month for magazine articles and the year, month, and day for newspaper articles).
◆ For titles of books, chapters in books, and journal articles, capitalize only the first word of the title and of the subtitle (if any) as well as any proper names.
◆ Give the issue number of the journal if the article cited is paginated by issue.
◆ Italicize the volume number of a journal article and the title of a book or a journal.
◆ Give the city and state of a book's publisher, using the postal abbreviations listed in Exhibit 15.
◆ However, major cities in the United States (such as Baltimore, Boston, Chicago, Dallas, Los Angeles, New York, Philadelphia, and San Francisco) can be listed without a state abbreviation.
◆ If you are listing a foreign city other than Amsterdam, Jerusalem, London, Milan, Moscow, New Delhi, Paris, Rome, Stockholm, Tokyo, or Vienna, then list the country as well.

Using these rules and the notes and examples below, you should encounter few problems. If you experience a problem, you might be able to generalize from these rules and notes or find an answer on the APA *Publication Manual* Web site (http://www.apastyle.org). Remember that the APA rule of thumb in all cases is to be clear, consistent, and complete in referencing source material:

Authored Book

Single author
Invert the author's name, using initials for the first and middle names, and give the year of publication, the italicized title of the book (capitalizing the first word of the title and subtitle), and the location and name of the publisher.

> Kimmel, A. J. (1996). *Ethical issues in behavioral research: A survey.*
> Cambridge, MA: Blackwell.

More than one author
Same as above, but insert a comma followed by an ampersand (&) before the last author's name.

> Shadish, W. R., Cook, T. D., & Campbell, D. T. (2001). *Experimental
> and quasi-experimental designs for generalized causal inference.*
> Boston: Houghton Mifflin.

EXHIBIT 15 **Postal abbreviations for states and territories**

Location	Abbreviation	Location	Abbreviation
Alabama	AL	Montana	MT
Alaska	AK	Nebraska	NE
Arizona	AZ	Nevada	NV
Arkansas	AR	New Hampshire	NH
California	CA	New Jersey	NJ
Colorado	CO	New Mexico	NM
Connecticut	CT	New York	NY
Delaware	DE	North Carolina	NC
District of Columbia	DC	North Dakota	ND
Florida	FL	Ohio	OH
Georgia	GA	Oklahoma	OK
Guam	GU	Oregon	OR
Hawaii	HI	Pennsylvania	PA
Idaho	ID	Puerto Rico	PR
Illinois	IL	Rhode Island	RI
Indiana	IN	South Carolina	SC
Iowa	IA	South Dakota	SD
Kansas	KS	Tennessee	TN
Kentucky	KY	Texas	TX
Louisiana	LA	Utah	UT
Maine	ME	Vermont	VT
Maryland	MD	Virginia	VA
Massachusetts	MA	Virgin Islands	VI
Michigan	MI	Washington	WA
Minnesota	MN	West Virginia	WV
Mississippi	MS	Wisconsin	WI
Missouri	MO	Wyoming	WY

Institutional author and publisher are the same

Give the full name of the institution, and list the publisher's name as "Author" when it is the same as the institutional author.

> American Psychiatric Association. (1994). *Diagnostic and statistical manual of mental disorders* (4th ed.). Washington, DC: Author.

Work in Press

Edited volume in production but not yet published

An edited volume that has been accepted by the publisher and is presumed to be in the process of production is considered in press. Insert in parentheses the abbreviation "Ed." (if one editor) or "Eds." (if more than one editor), followed by a period, and then write "in press" in parentheses, followed by a period.

> Pattanayak, B., & Gupta, V. (Eds.). (in press). *Creating performance organizations.* New Delhi: Sage.

Journal article accepted for publication but not yet in print
A manuscript that has been officially accepted for publication by the editor of a journal is considered in press, not merely a manuscript that has been submitted to a journal.

> Frei, R. L., Racicot, B., & Travagline, A. (in press). The impact of monochromic and type A behavior patterns on faculty research productivity and job-induced stress. *Journal of Managerial Psychology.*

Chapter in edited book in production but not yet in print
A chapter that has been accepted by the editor of a book that, in turn, has been accepted by the publisher is considered in press. Notice that the editors' names are not inverted, whereas the chapter authors' names are inverted as usual.

> Suls, J., & Martin, R. (in press). Social comparison processes in the physical health domain. In A. Baum, T. Revenson, & J. Singer (Eds.), *Handbook of health and psychology.* Mahwah, NJ: Erlbaum.

Authored book in production but not yet in print
A book manuscript that has been accepted by the publisher and is in the process of being prepared for publication is considered in press. Notice that the state as well as the city are listed in this illustration, the reason being that there is also a Cambridge in the United Kingdom.

> Fine, G. A. (in press). *Mushroom worlds: Naturework and the taming of the wild.* Cambridge, MA: Harvard University Press.

Monograph in a journal issue not yet in print
A monograph is a lengthy manuscript that the journal publishes either separately as a supplement or as a whole entire issue of the journal. This example refers to a monograph accepted by the editor, but not yet printed; once the monograph is published, the issue number and the supplement or part number (if it is published separately) are indicated in parentheses after the volume number.

> Lana, R. E. (in press). Choice and chance in the formation of society. *Journal of Mind and Behavior.*

Edited Published Work

Single editor of a book
After the editor's name, insert "Ed." in parentheses, followed by a period, the italicized title of the book, and so forth.

Morawski, J. G. (Ed.). (1988). *The rise of experimentation in American psychology.* New Haven, CT: Yale University Press.

More than one editor, more than one volume, revised edition
To indicate more than one editor, "Eds." is inserted in parentheses, followed by a period. The number of the edition and the number of volumes (and the abbreviation "Vols.," capitalized) are noted in parentheses after the title. If this were the first revised edition, then the abbreviation "Rev. ed." can be substituted for "2nd ed."

Gilbert, D. T., Fiske, S. T., & Lindzey, G. (Eds.). (1988). *The handbook of social psychology* (4th ed., Vols. 1-2). Boston: McGraw-Hill.

Work Republished at a Later Date

Book of collected work
The date that the original work appeared is included in parentheses after the full citation of the current edition.

Demosthenes. (1852). *The Olynthiac and other public orations of Demosthenes.* London: Henry G. Bohn. (Original work written 349 B.C.)

Single volume in multivolume series of collected work
The years in parentheses (1779/1971) indicate that the original work was published in 1779 and the current edition in 1971; the number of the particular volume in which the work appeared is indicated in parentheses after the title of the series.

Lessing, G. E. (1779/1971). *Gotthold Ephraim Lessing: Werke* (Vol. 2). München, Germany: Carl Hanser Verlag.

Chapter in an anthology
The years in parentheses (1733/1903) indicate the date of publication of the original work and the anthology. The pages on which the work appears in the anthology are indicated in parentheses after the title of the anthology, followed by a period.

Pope, A. (1733/1903). Moral essays: Epistle I. To Sir Richard Temple, Lord Cobham, of the knowledge and character of men. In H. W. Boynton (Ed.), *The complete poetical works of Pope* (pp. 157-160). Boston: Houghton Mifflin.

Article or Chapter

Article by a single author in journal paginated by volume
The journal name and volume (*42*) are written in italics, followed by the page numbers (97-108, not in italics) of the article.

Scott-Jones, D. (1994). Ethical issues in reporting and referring in research with low-income minority children. *Ethics and Behavior, 42,*
97-108.

Article by five authors in journal paginated by volume
An ampersand (&) is placed before the last author's name, and only the journal name and volume are italicized.

Gabrieli, J. D. E., Fleischman, D. A., Keane, M. M., Reminger, S. L., &
Morrell, F. (1995). Double dissociation between memory systems
underlying explicit and implicit memory in the human brain. *Psychological Science, 6,* 76-82.

More than six authors
If there are seven or more authors, only the first six are listed, followed by a
comma and "et al." (no ampersand).

Thomas, C. B., Hall, J. A., Miller, F. D., Dewhirst, J. R., Fine, G. A.,
Taylor, M., et al. (1979). Evaluation apprehension, social desirability,
and the interpretation of test correlations. *Social Behavior and Personality, 7,* 193-197.

Chapter in edited book
The authors' names are inverted, but not the editors' names. The page numbers of the chapter (pp. 130-165) are placed in parentheses immediately after
the italicized title of the book, followed by a period.

Aditya, R. N., House, R. J., & Kerr, S. (2000). Theory and practice of
leadership: Into the new millennium. In C. L. Cooper & E. A. Locke
(Eds.), *Industrial and organizational psychology: Linking theory and
practice* (pp. 130-165). Cambridge, MA: Blackwell.

Chapter author with hyphenated first and last names
Hyphens in the first name and last name are retained, with all other information presented as before.

Perret-Clermont, A.-N., Perret, J.-F., & Bell, N. (1991). The social construction of meaning and cognitive ability in elementary school children. In L. Resnick, J. M. Levine, & S. B. Teasley (Eds.), *Perspectives
on socially shared cognition* (pp. 41-62). Washington, DC: American
Psychological Association.

Entry in encyclopedia paginated by volume
The volume and page numbers of the entry are indicated in parentheses after
the italicized title of the encyclopedia. Unusual in this example is that there
were two publishers of the encyclopedia, both (as indicated) located in the
same city.

Stanley, J. C. (1971). Design of controlled experiments in education. In L. C. Deighton (Ed.), *The encyclopedia of education* (Vol. 3, pp. 474-483). New York: Macmillan and Free Press.

Article in newsletter paginated by issue
Immediately after the italicized volume number (*23*), the issue number is indicated (4, no italics) in parentheses.

Camara, W. J. (2001). Do accommodations improve or hinder psychometric qualities of assessment? *The Score Newsletter, 23*(4), 4-6.

Article in journal paginated by issue
Same as above.

Valdiserri, R. O., Tama, G. M., & Ho, M. (1988). The role of community advisory committees in clinical trials of anti-HIV agents. *IRB: A Review of Human Subjects Research, 10*(4), 5-7.

Non-English Publication

Book
Diacritical marks (an umlaut in this example) and capital letters are used for non-English words in the same way they were used in the original language. The English translation of the book's title is included in brackets immediately after the German title, followed by a period.

Gniech, G. (1976). *Störeffekte in psychologischen Experimenten* [Artifacts in psychological experiments]. Stuttgart, Germany: Verlag W. Kohlhammer.

Journal article
The same rule referring to the use of diacritical marks and capital letters applies to the non-English title of the article and the name of the journal.

Foa, U. G. (1966). Le nombre huit dans la socialization de l'enfant [The number eight in the socialization of the infant]. *Bulletin du Centre d'Études et Recherches Psychologiques, 15*, 39-47.

Chapter in Multivolume Edited Series

Different author and editor
Volume and page numbers of the chapter are indicated in parentheses after the italicized series title.

Kipnis, D. (1984). The use of power in organizations and interpersonal settings. In S. Oskamp (Ed.), *Applied social psychology* (Vol. 5, pp. 171-210). Newbury Park, CA: Sage.

Same author and editor
Notice that the chapter author's name is inverted, but the same name is not inverted when the author is also the editor of the series in which the chapter appears.

> Koch, S. (1959). General introduction to the series. In S. Koch (Ed.), *Psychology: A study of a science* (Vol. 1, pp. 1-18). New York: McGraw-Hill.

Mass Media Article

Magazine article
In parentheses followed by a period, the year and month(s) (if published monthly) and the day (if published more frequently than monthly) are indicated. If the volume number is known, then it is indicated as shown here in italics (29), followed by the page numbers.

> Csikszentmihalyi, M. (1996, July/August). The creative personality. *Psychology Today, 29*, 36-40.

Newspaper article (author listed)
All the page numbers are indicated for an article that appears on discontinuous pages, and the page numbers are separated by a comma.

> Grady, D. (1999, October 11). Too much of a good thing? Doctor challenges drug manual. *The New York Times*, Section F, pp. 1, 2.

Newspaper article (no author listed)
When no author's name is listed in a newspaper article, the work is referenced by the title of the article and alphabetized in the list of references by the first significant word in the title ("toast").

> A toast to Newton and a long-lived "Principia." (1999, October 11). *The New York Times*, Section F, p. 4.

Dictionary or Encyclopedia

Dictionary (no author listed)
When no author's name is listed on the title page of a dictionary or an encyclopedia, the work is referenced by the title of the work and alphabetized by the first significant word in the title.

> *Random House dictionary of the English language.* (1966). New York: Random House.

Encyclopedia (more than one volume, two publishers in two locations)
After the name of the general editor of the encyclopedia, "Ed." is inserted in parentheses, followed by a period. The number of volumes appears in

parentheses following the title and then a period. In this case, the title page of the encyclopedia lists two publishers in two locations.

> Kazdin, A. E. (Ed.). (2000). *Encyclopedia of psychology* (Vols. 1-8). Washington, DC: American Psychological Association. New York: Oxford University Press.

Doctoral Dissertation or Master's Thesis

Doctoral dissertation abstract
The *DAI* (*Dissertation Abstracts International*) volume and page number of the abstract are indicated, ending with a period.

> Esposito, J. (1987). Subjective factors and rumor transmission: A field investigation of the influence of anxiety, importance, and belief on rumormongering (Doctoral dissertation, Temple University, 1986). *Dissertation Abstracts International, 48,* 596B.

Unpublished doctoral dissertation
If a manuscript copy of the dissertation was used and the *DAI* number is not known, or if an abstract was not published in *DAI*, write "Unpublished doctoral dissertation" and give the university and location.

> Mettetal, G. W. (1982). The conversation of female friends at three ages: The importance of fantasy, gossip, and self-disclosure. Unpublished doctoral dissertation, University of Illinois, Urbana.

Master's thesis (outside the United States)
If a manuscript copy of the master's thesis was used and the *MAI* (*Master's Abstracts International*) number is not known, or if an abstract was not published in *MAI*, state "Unpublished master's thesis" and the college or university and location. In this case, observe that the title contains a British spelling ("organisational"), which a spell check program might try to "correct."

> Hunt, E. (2000). *Correlates of uncertainty during organisational change.* Unpublished master's thesis, University of Queensland, St. Lucia, Queensland, Australia.

Unpublished Material

Technical report
The title of a technical report is italicized, followed by the report number in parentheses and the location and name of the organization that issued the report.

> LoSciuto, L. A., Aiken, L. S., & Ausetts, M. A. (1979). *Professional and paraprofessional drug abuse counselors: Three reports* (DHEW Publication No. 79-858). Rockville, MD: National Institute on Drug Abuse.

Unpublished manuscript
The title of an unpublished manuscript is indicated in italics, followed by "Unpublished manuscript" and the institution and its location.

> Burnham, J. R. (1966). *Experimenter bias and lesion labeling.* Unpublished manuscript, Purdue University, West Lafayette, IN.

Manuscript submitted for publication (but not yet accepted)
If a manuscript submitted for publication has not been formally accepted by the editor, then the name of the journal or book publisher to whom the manuscript was submitted should not be displayed. No matter whether the submitted manuscript is for a book, a chapter, or a journal article, the title of the manuscript is italicized.

> Mithalal, C. (2002). *Protocols of telephone therapy.* Manuscript submitted for publication.

Paper (unpublished) presented at a meeting
The month of the meeting is listed, the title of the paper is italicized, and the name of the sponsoring organization and location of the meeting are indicated.

> Rajala, A. K., DeNicolis, J. L., Brecher, E. G., & Hantula, D. A (1995, May). *Investing in occupational safety: A utility analysis perspective.* Paper presented at the annual meeting of the Eastern Academy of Management, Ithaca, NY.

Poster presented at a meeting
Same as above.

> Freeman, M. A. (1995, August). *Demographic correlates of individualism and collectivism: A study of social values in Sri Lanka.* Poster presented at the annual meeting of the American Psychological Society, New York.

Audiovisual Media

Motion picture
After each primary contributor, the particular contribution is noted in parentheses, and "Motion picture" is inserted in brackets after the italicized title of the film. The country of origin (where the film was primarily made or released) and the motion picture studio are indicated.

> Zinneman, F. (Director), & Foreman, C. (Screenwriter). (1952). *High noon* [Motion picture]. United States: Universal Artists.

Television broadcast
The key here is simply to provide sufficient information to identify the broadcast as best you can, without leaving out any significant identifying detail.

Doyle, W. (Producer). (2001, November 3). *An American insurrection* [Television broadcast]. New York: C-Span 2.

Music recording

The information in this example includes the artist's name, the date of copyright, the title of the piece, the recording artist, the title of the album *(Mahler–Bernstein)*, the medium of recording (CD, record, cassette, etc.), and the location.

Mahler, G. (1991). Symphonie No. 8. [Recorded by L. Bernstein & Wiener Philharmoniker]. On *Mahler–Bernstein* [CD]. Hamburg, Germany: Deutsche Grammophon.

Electronic Sources

Some of the more common types of electronic references are illustrated below. However, because new developments in the electronic media are in a constant state of flux, the APA regularly updates its electronic referencing Web site. If you have a specific reference that is not covered by the examples below, or a citation in text of electronic material that was not previously covered, go to the following APA Web site for more detailed information: http://www.apastyle.org/elecref.html

Abstract retrieved from PsycINFO

The article is cited in the usual way, but the fact that only the abstract (not the full text) was retrieved is indicated, followed by the date it was retrieved and the Web source.

Morgeson, F. P., Seligman, M. E., Sternberg, R. J., Taylor, S. E., & Manning, C. M. (1999). Lessons learned from a life in psychological science: Implications for young scientists. *American Psychologist, 54,* 106-116. Abstract retrieved October 14, 1999, from PsycINFO database.

Full-text article retrieved from PsycARTICLES

Same as above, except for the omission of "Abstract" in the retrieval information.

Egeth, H. E. (1993). What do we *not* know about eyewitness identification? *American Psychologist, 48,* 577-580. Retrieved January 14, 2002, from PsycARTICLES.

Same article retrieved electronically (another option)

Another suitable option when referencing articles retrieved electronically is to add the words "Electronic version" in brackets after the title, followed by a period, and then the full citation of the printed version.

Egeth, H. E. (1993). What do we *not* know about eyewitness identification? [Electronic version]. *American Psychologist, 48,* 577-580.

Article in Internet-only journal
Whenever possible, the URL that links to the article is indicated. If the URL stretches to another line, then it should be broken after a slash or before a period, but do not insert a hyphen at the break.

> Lassiter, G. D., Munhall, P. J., Geers, A. L., Handley, I. M., & Weiland, P. E. (2001, November 1). Criminal confessions on videotape: Does camera perspective bias their perceived veracity? *Current Research in Social Psychology, 2,* 15-22. Retrieved November 2, 2001, from www.uiowa.edu/~grpproc/crisp/crisp.7.1.htm

Information retrieved from Web site
The host or institutional provider of this information is listed, followed by the date of the document or information (in parentheses, followed by a period), and then the title of the document or information, and finally the date retrieved and the URL.

> American Psychological Association. (1999). Scholarships, grants and funding opportunities. Retrieved October 14, 1999, www.apa.org/ students/grants.html

Proofing and Correcting

We now come to the final steps before you submit your paper: proofing and correcting. Read the finished paper more than once. Ask yourself the following questions:

- ◆ Are there omissions?
- ◆ Are there misspellings?
- ◆ Are the numbers correct?
- ◆ Are the hyphenations correct?
- ◆ Do all the references cited in the body of the paper also appear in the references section?

The first time you read your final draft, the appeal of the neat, clean copy may lead you to overlook errors. Put the paper aside for 24 hours, and then read it carefully again. After you have corrected any errors, give the paper a final look, checking to be sure all the pages are there and in order. If you adhered to the guidelines in this manual, you should have the sense of a job well done and should feel confident that the paper will receive the serious attention that a clear, consistent, and attractive manuscript deserves.

CREATING POSTERS AND BRIEF REPORTS

The poster is a visual display used to convey the nature and major findings of your research in the setting of a public forum. The convention in this forum is also to provide interested people with a handout that describes the research. The exercise of boiling down your research to its most pertinent components, without sacrificing valuable details, will teach you the art of selecting critical information.

Posters and Handout Reports

It is becoming increasingly common for students not only to prepare a detailed written report of their findings, but also to present their results in poster form. Some posters may even be presented at conferences, such as at the regional and specialized meetings listed in the *American Psychologist* each month. This format has its own set of conventions and requirements, although they are not uniform. Instead, they depend on the parameters set forth by the organizers of each specific conference. The *American Psychologist* lists Web sites you can visit for detailed information and also lists e-mail addresses where you can direct questions that are not answered on the Web sites.

If you can, it is a good idea to attend a poster session. In this way, you can assess the visual impact of the various presentations. Which posters draw your eye? What is it about some posters that makes them more visually accessible than others? Poster presenters planning to do further research, or planning to write up their results for submission to a journal, find the feedback they obtain invaluable. Without drawing people to the poster, however, there is no opportunity for feedback or discussion. Thus, it is important to create a poster that is visually inviting, and in this chapter, we provide guidelines to help you.

To supplement the information that is visually presented in the poster, a concise handout is also usually prepared. The report you prepared for class would be inappropriate as a handout. It is too costly to reproduce a lot of copies of a lengthy paper (the APA asks poster presenters to bring along 50 copies of the research report). Moreover, the paper you wrote for a course contains more information than anyone but your instructor will want to know. Thus, we also illustrate how to condense Jane's detailed research report in Appendix B into a brief report for distribution.

Guidelines for the Poster

The way a poster session usually works is that you are asked to show up with your material in a large room or auditorium area, where you will see rows of display boards. Assuming you have not been assigned a particular board, it is first-come, first-served—so be sure to arrive early. Pushpins and Velcro hooks are usually available for attaching the pages to the display board. Some presenters, in advance of the meeting, have arranged and pasted their pages on a cardboard poster, and they simply attach the whole poster to the display board. To be safe, it is a good idea to bring extra pushpins. You are not allowed to write, paint, or use paste on the display board, and you must have your display set up in the time allotted (10 minutes, for example), and then removed and the display board left neat and presentable for the next set of presenters.

Exhibit 16 illustrates how guidelines for poster presentations can differ from one organization to another. The exhibit provides a comparison of poster elements distributed by the American Psychological Association (APA) and the American Association for the Advancement of Science (AAAS). Notice that, in virtually every respect, there is some difference. For example, the AAAS's poster board surface is two feet wider than the APA's; the larger the surface, the more the information that can be displayed. The APA guidelines recommend that an abstract of no more than 300 words be posted in the upper-left corner of the board surface, whereas the AAAS guidelines suggest that the sequence of information begin with the major conclusions.

It is impossible in this book to anticipate every special requirement you may encounter, but you can ensure that your poster will be suitable by finding out the requirements before you begin to design it. To help you get started, Exhibit 17 shows a compact template for a poster of only six $8\frac{1}{2} \times 11$-inch pages and space for the title, author(s), and affiliation heading at the top. The material, allowing for some spacing between the pages and the heading, could be fitted onto a surface approximately 2 feet high and a little over 3 feet wide. The poster board surface furnished by the APA and the AAAS (Exhibit 16) allows the presenter more room to accommodate essential information, whereas Exhibit 17 illustrates how the research can be condensed when there is less space available.

As you design your poster, remember that what you are trying to accomplish is to draw attention to your study. You also want to chat with people who are interested in learning more about it, as well as to ferret out issues and ideas that can help you anticipate problems if you expect to submit the

EXHIBIT 16   APA *and* AAAS *poster design suggestions*

Poster Element	APA	AAAS
Poster board surface	4' high, 6' wide	4' high, 8' wide
Legibility	At a 3' distance or more	About a 5' distance
Sequence	Abstract (300 words or less) in upper-left corner, followed by ordered material (use numbers, letters, or arrows)	Conclusions, then supporting text, ending with brief summary
Title and author(s)	1" high, at least	2–3" high
Lettering of text	⅜" high, preferably boldface font, or hand-lettered with regular felt tip pen	24-point font, but can also use color as well as different sizes and proportions
Section headings	Label headings clearly	½–1" high subheadings
Tables and figures	Make them simple, clear, and easily visible	Graphics are preferable to tables
Handouts	50 copies, full paper	Abstract (number unspecified)

research to a journal or to continue doing research on this topic. One instructor told us that he cautioned students to be prepared for being in a cramped area with relatively poor lighting, a lot of distracting noise, and other sensory activity.

Here are three tips to keep in mind:

◆ Choose a font size that is big enough for tired, middle-aged viewers with failing eyesight to see from a distance.
◆ Keep the tables and figures simple, because people don't usually want to stand around and study them.
◆ Keeping it simple also means being selective in what you report, although it doesn't mean being evasive or misleading—only straightforward and concise.

Besides reviewing the specifics in Exhibit 16 and any information provided by the organizer of your poster session, here are further tips on how to format the poster:

◆ Use a typeface that is easy to read, such as Arial or Times New Roman, not a fancy one that has squiggles or loops.
◆ Make sure that your font size is visible at a distance, such as 24 points (one-quarter inch high; as recommended by the AAAS) or even 32 points.
◆ Don't overcomplicate tables or figures, and don't use jargon or exotic terms that are likely to be unfamiliar to your viewers.
◆ Use color for important highlights, but use it sparingly because you are reporting a scientific study, not creating a work of art.

EXHIBIT 17   *Template for a six-page poster*

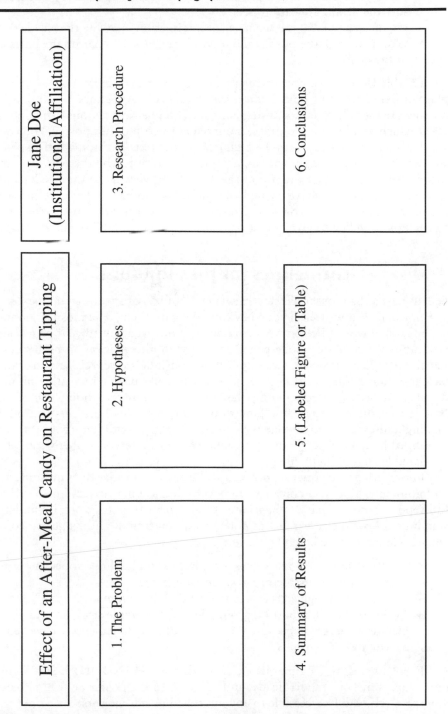

◆ Make your figures and illustrations bold and self-explanatory, and be sure the details are easy to see.
◆ Organize and label the sequence of information in a way that leads the viewer through the poster, and leave some space to separate the parts of the poster.

Exhibit 18 shows sample text material for a poster using the six-page template in Exhibit 17 and Jane Doe's research report in Appendix B. All that is missing are the title of Jane's poster, her name, and her institutional affiliation, all of which would be in boldface, mounted at the top of her poster. You can see that Jane's poster captures the highlights of her research study. If the sponsor requires that you begin with an abstract (as suggested by the APA), try to make it succinct, and let the rest of the poster lead viewers to the results and conclusions. Once you have created your poster, stand back a few feet and see if you can read it easily. You will also want to show it to your instructor, and to any others willing to give honest opinions about its readability and design.

Guidelines for the Handout

Because even the most interested viewers are unlikely to want to take extensive notes, have a written report they can take with them. The most economical approach would be to try to confine vital information to two pages, so you can make copies of a one-page handout with information on both sides. Exhibit 19 illustrates such a handout based on Jane's research. If you compare it with her full report in Appendix B, you will observe how superfluous details have been excised and only the most essential information is included. Notice that there is space for Jane to provide her e-mail and institutional mailing address, should anyone wish to communicate with her about this research. Although the poster did not contain a list of references, there is an abbreviated list in the handout.

In preparing your brief report, you will want to consider the same criteria and guidelines that you consulted in developing the major sections of your full report. Your primary obligation is to give people a clear, precise understanding of how the research was done, what you found, and what you concluded. Here are three helpful guidelines:

◆ Try to anticipate people's questions. For example, think about the comments your instructor wrote on your paper.
◆ Tell people enough so they can make up their own minds.
◆ At the very least, report (a) group means, (b) sample sizes, and (c) measurement error, because these minimal raw ingredients are needed to reanalyze the results.

Finally, bring along a manila envelope, labeled HANDOUTS. Slip 50 or more copies of your report inside, and attach it to the poster board, making your research readily accessible to any interested poster viewers.

EXHIBIT 18   *Sample poster content*

---

1. The Problem

Empirical studies have found that the following techniques used by servers in restaurants can increase tipping:

- touching the recipient of the check on the palm of the hand for a fraction of a second
- giving customers sitting alone a large, open-mouth smile
- squatting to the eye level of customers
- telling customers one's first name during the initial visit
- drawing a happy face or writing "thank you" on the check.

All seem to have in common that servers are doing something that also increases customers' impressions of friendliness. In this study, another such technique was experimentally manipulated—offering customers an after-meal miniature chocolate candy.

---

2. Hypotheses

- It was predicted that merely offering customers an after-meal candy when presenting the check would increase tipping, and that offering them two pieces of candy would further increase tipping.

- Because people generally feel obligated to reciprocate when they receive an unexpected favor, it was predicted that creating an impression that the offer of a second candy reflected the server's generous impulse would produce the highest tips.

EXHIBIT 18 *Continued*

---

3. Research Procedure

The study involved 80 dining parties in an upscale restaurant in New Jersey, who were randomly assigned to the following conditions:

* *Control condition:* The server presented the check to customers at the end of the meal.

* *1-piece condition:* When presenting the check, the server had a basket of assorted miniature chocolates and offered each person 1 candy.

* *2-piece condition:* When presenting the check, the server offered each person 2 candies.

* *1 + 1 condition:* When presenting the check, the server offered 1 candy and said, "Oh, have another piece"—implying a generous afterthought.

---

4. Summary of Results

* As the Table of Results indicates, the pattern of tipping increased in the predicted direction, rising from the control to 1-piece to 2-piece to 1 + 1 conditions.

* A linear contrast was highly significant ($p < .0001$), and the 95% confidence interval for the effect size ranged from $r = .45$ to $.73$.

* The t-tests comparing (a) the control and 2-piece conditions and (b) the control and 1 + 1 conditions were significant ($p < .0001$ one-tailed), both effect size rs $> .5$.

* The t-test comparing the control and no-candy conditions was not significant ($p = .17$ one-tailed, $r_{effect\ size} = .15$), but power was less than .5.

EXHIBIT 18   *Continued*

---

5. Table of Results

Mean Tip Percentage, Standard Deviation, and Sample Size

	Treatment condition			
Results	No candy	1 piece	2 pieces	1 + 1 pieces
M	18.95	19.59	21.62	22.99
SD	1.46	1.71	2.45	2.43
n	20	20	20	20

Note. Mean (*M*) value refers to average tip percentage in each condition. Tip percentage for each dining party was calculated by dividing the tip amount by the bill amount before taxes, then multiplying by 100. The standard deviation (*SD*) refers to the variability of *n* = 20 tip percentages around the mean value.

---

6. Conclusions

• Offering customers an after-meal candy can increase tip percentages, and two candies increases tips more than one candy. This finding is consistent with the idea that a token gift conveys friendliness, and that, in return, people give larger tips as a sign of their appreciation.

• Results in the 1 + 1 condition imply the role of reciprocity in increasing tips, in that people gave the largest tip percentages after being led to believe they were benefiting from the server's generous impulse.

• Further research is needed, however, to determine the generalizability of these findings to other servers, other types of restaurants, and other areas. Research is also needed to confirm the presumed mediational role of "friendliness" and "generosity" in the study.

EXHIBIT 19   *Sample brief report for distribution*

Effect of an After-Meal Candy on Restaurant Tipping

Jane Doe[*]
(Institutional affiliation and/or mailing address for correspondence)
(e-mail address)

*This brief report is based on a poster of the same title, which was presented at
(name of meeting, date of presentation, location of meeting).*

Background and Hypotheses

More than 1 million people in the United States work as waiters and waitresses.
Although they usually receive wages from their employers, the major source of income for servers comes in the form of tips from customers. Research studies have
demonstrated techniques for encouraging tipping, including (a) touching customers
twice on the palm of the hand for a fraction of a second (Hornik, 1992); (b) giving
customers sitting alone a large, open-mouth smile (Tidd & Lockard, 1978); (c) squatting to the eye level of customers (Lynn & Mynier, 1993); (d) introducing oneself by
one's first name at the initial visit (Garrity & Degelman, 1990); and (e) writing
"thank you" or drawing a happy face on the check (Rind & Bordia, 1995, 1996).

These techniques seem to have in common that the servers are doing something that may also increase customers' impressions of friendliness. In this study, another technique along this line was experimentally evaluated, guided by the
following three hypotheses:
1. When presenting the check, merely offering customers an after-meal candy
will increase tipping.
2. On the assumption this effect is cumulative, offering two pieces of candy
will further increase tipping.
3. Because people generally feel obligated to reciprocate when they receive
a favor (cf. Regan, 1971), creating the impression that the offer of a second candy
is a favor reflecting the server's own generous impulse will produce the largest tipping percentage.

Method

A total of 80 dining parties in an upscale Italian-American restaurant in New
Jersey were assigned at random to one of four conditions, 20 units per condition. In
the *control condition*, the server simply presented the check to the customers at the
end of the meal. In the three other conditions, the server was given a basket of
miniature chocolates to take with her when presenting the check: In the *1-piece condition*, she offered each person in the dining party 1 candy of his or her choice. In
the *2-piece condition*, she offered each person 2 candies. In the *1 + 1 condition*, she
offered a candy and then said, "Oh, have another piece," to create the impression of
a generous afterthought.

Results

The dependent measure was defined as the tip percentage—that is, the tip amount
divided by the amount of the bill before taxes, which was then multiplied by 100.
Based on the hypotheses, the overall prediction was that the average tip percentage in
the four groups would increase from control to 1-piece to 2-piece to 1 + 1 conditions.

---

[*] I thank Dr. Bruce Rind for providing me with valuable guidance throughout this research project, and also
thank the owner of the restaurant and the server for making it possible for me to carry out this research.

EXHIBIT 19   Continued

Results indicated that the pattern of tip percentages was exactly as predicted. The average value was (a) 18.95% ($SD = 1.46$) in the control, (b) 19.59% ($SD = 1.71$) in the 1-piece condition, (c) 21.62% ($SD = 2.45$) in the 2-piece condition, and (d) 22.99% ($SD = 2.43$) in the 1 + 1 condition. A linear contrast (with lambda weights of -3, -1, +1, +3, respectively) was highly significant and the effect size large, $F(1, 76) = 44.97$, $p < .0001$, $r_{effect size} = .61$ (95% confidence interval ranged from $r_{effect size} = .45$ to .73).

Independent t tests comparing the control and the other three conditions, using $MSE = 4.45$ and $df = 76$, were significant only for the (a) control vs. 2-piece comparison ($t = 3.99$, $p < .0001$, $r_{effect size} = .54$) and (b) control vs. 1 + 1 comparison ($t = 6.05$, $p < .0001$, $r_{effect size} = .61$). The control vs. 1-piece comparison, with statistical power less than .5, resulted in $t = .95$, $p = .17$ one-tailed, $r_{effect size} = .15$.

Conclusions

The pattern of tip percentages (and the linear contrast) is consistent with the idea that offering a token gift of candy to customers can increase tip percentages, and offering two candies is better than offering one candy. The theoretical explanation may be that offering people a token gift conveys a sense of friendliness, in return for which they respond amiably by rewarding the server with a larger tip. Results in the 1 + 1 condition implied the role of reciprocity, as customers responded with the largest tips when they were led to believe they were recipients of the server's personal generosity.

Because only one waitress participated in this study, research is needed to establish the generalizability of the findings to male servers as well as to other female servers, other types of restaurants, and other areas. Further research is also needed to confirm the presumed role of "friendliness" and "generosity."

References

Garrity, K., & Degelman, D. (1990). Effect of server introduction on restaurant tipping. *Journal of Applied Social Psychology, 20,* 168-172.

Hornik, J. (1992). Tactile stimulation and consumer response. *Journal of Consumer Research, 19,* 449-458.

Lynn, M., & Mynier, K. (1993). Effect of server posture on restaurant tipping. *Journal of Applied Social Psychology, 23,* 678-685.

Regan, D. T. (1971). Effects of a favor and liking on compliance. *Journal of Experimental Social Psychology, 7,* 627-639.

Rind, B., & Bordia, P. (1995). Effect of server's "thank you" and personalization on restaurant tipping. *Journal of Applied Social Psychology, 25,* 745-751.

Rind, B., & Bordia, P. (1996). Effect of restaurant tipping of male and female servers drawing a happy, smiling face on the backs of customers' checks. *Journal of Applied Social Psychology, 26,* 218-225.

Tidd, K., & Lockard, J. (1978). Monetary significance of the affiliative smile: A case for reciprocal altruism. *Bulletin of the Psychometric Society, 11,* 344-346.

A

SAMPLE ESSAY

Pages are numbered consecutively, beginning with the title page, and contain a short heading of two or three words from the title.

Perspectives on Intelligence   1

Two Major Perspectives on Human Intelligence

The title is double-spaced in uppercase and lowercase letters and centered between the left and right margins.

The student's name is centered, two double-spaced lines below the title.

John Smith

Psychology 222

Instructor: Prof. Anne Skleder

(Date the Term Paper is Submitted)

The course number, the instructor's name, and the date the paper is submitted are double-spaced.

The abstract
begins on a
new page.

The abstract
is not
indented.

Perspectives on Intelligence   2

Abstract

The purpose of this paper is to compare two major perspectives on the nature of

human intelligence. Traditionally, in psychology, human intelligence has been

regarded as g-centric, meaning that a general trait (labeled g) is believed to be a

component of every valid measure of intelligence. In contrast to this classic idea is

what I describe as the *multiplex view,* by which I mean the more recently developed

idea that there are several kinds of intelligence that do not necessarily have a

common psychometric core. One leading multiplex theory is that formulated by

Howard Gardner, which is a focal point in this discussion. Two criticisms of

multiplex theories of intelligence are examined, and the paper concludes with a

broad overview of the direction of recent work in this area.

The term g
is italicized
(or
underlined).

In an essay, the
abstract tells
why the paper was
written and, very
briefly, what the
paper argues or
explains in the
context of its purpose.

The first line of every paragraph in the text is indented five to seven spaces.

The text begins on a new page and opens by repeating the title.

Perspectives on Intelligence   3

Two Major Perspectives on Human Intelligence

People use the word *intelligence* and its various synonyms in many different ways to refer to distinct aptitudes. Some individuals are called *book smart,* a term meaning that they are strong in verbal or mathematical aptitudes. Others are referred to as *street smart,* a term implying that they are intellectually shrewd in the ways of the world. Still others are said to have *business savvy* or *political sense* or the ability to *read people like a book,* phrases meaning that their skills involve interpersonal aptitude that may not be directly measured by standard tests of intelligence. This paper examines the nature of human intelligence from two major perspectives. One view is frequently characterized as the *g-centric view* because it reflects the psychometric idea of a general trait (g) that is presumed to be at the core of human intelligence. The second major view, which is more recent, is characterized here as the *multiplex view* because it reflects the assumption of multiple intelligences housed within the same culture (but not necessarily in any single individual within the culture). I begin by elaborating on the distinction between these two perspectives and then focus on one prominent example of the multiplex view, the work of Howard Gardner (1983, 1985). Two main criticisms of multiplex theories are examined, and the paper concludes with an overview of what I perceive as the direction of current work in this area.

Defined scientific and technical terms are italicized.

Although the left margin is even, the right margin is ragged.

Two General Conceptions of Intelligence

The Traditional View

For much of the 20th century, psychological research on intelligence focused on the existence of a general overriding trait of intelligence, usually measured by

First-level headings are centered, whereas second-level headings are flush left and in italics (or underlined).

All the major sections of the text follow each other without a break.

Leave a margin of at least 1 inch on all four sides, providing room for the reader's comments.

various short-answer tests of mathematical and linguistic skills. Influenced by the theoretical and psychometric contributions of Charles Spearman (1927), who regarded intelligence as a general characteristic, psychological and educational researchers in the intelligence test movement have accepted as valid the *g*-centric (or *g*-centered) idea of intelligence. A number of psychometricians, such as Arthur Jensen (1969), have further argued that differences in *g* can be attributed largely to heritability (genetic factors) as opposed to environmental or cultural influences, a position that has been contested in psychology and education.

Use a 12-point typeface, preferably Times New Roman or Courier.

Regarding the essential idea of a general characteristic of intelligence, child development researchers inspired by the theoretical and empirical work of Jean Piaget have also argued for the idea of general structures of the mind (Siegler & Richards, 1982). These structures, they have asserted, develop in a similar way in all children. In the biological area, some investigators have attempted to operationalize *g* by measuring the speed of neural transmission (Reed & Jensen, 1992) or by using measures of hemispheric localization (Levy, 1974). In the 1990s, a controversial reanalysis of IQ test data by Herrnstein and Murray (1994), in a book entitled *The Bell Curve*, ignited a spirited debate about the presumed role of *g* in the lives of individuals and in the larger social order.

An ampersand (&) appears in parentheses, where "and" is used otherwise.

Book titles are italicized.

Although the traditional view of intelligence has been periodically challenged, many experts consider fundamental the idea that standard IQ tests provide magical numbers that allow us to distinguish "bright" people from the "not-so-bright" in terms of accrued knowledge or potential for learning. Thus, whether psychologists and educators mean by *intelligence* (a) the ability to adapt to the environment, (b)

The list is lettered for clarity.

the ability to deal with symbols or abstractions, or (c) the ability to learn, many experts assume that a core ingredient in these aptitudes is the factor known as g (Gilbert, 1971).

One early criticism of this view was articulated by L. L. Thurstone (1938) and his coworkers. On the basis of psychometric studies they conducted with large numbers of participants, Thurstone and Thurstone (1941) concluded that there are distinct aptitudes, which they called "primary mental abilities," and which include verbal comprehension, word fluency, numerical ability, and spatial relations. More recently, Sternberg and Berg (1986) reported that a panel of experts had embraced diverse, and ostensibly divergent, factors in what they theoretically associated with intelligence. Controversy surrounds the meaning of intelligence as well as its relation to real-world skills, but a task force of the American Psychological Association (APA) nevertheless was able to agree on a list of "knowns" about intelligence (Neisser et al., 1996).

Abbreviations are spelled out first.

The Multiplex View

In his 1967 book, J. P. Guilford developed the theory that ordinary intelligence encompasses multiple aptitudes and, in turn, raised the possibility that there are over a hundred different ways in which individuals can excel intellectually. Moving the idea of multiple abilities in still another direction, Robert Sternberg (1990)--1 of 11 coauthors of the APA report by Neisser et al. (1996)--also argued that the nature of the information processing measured by standard IQ tests is actually quite different from that involved in certain kinds of complex reasoning in everyday life. By way of illustration, Ceci and Liker (1986) reported that skill in handicapping racehorses

Single-digit number that is part of a group is not written as "one."

The first
full
citation
of a work
lists up
to five
authors.

Perspectives on Intelligence   6

could not be predicted from handicappers' performance on the Wechsler Adult

Intelligence Scale. Sternberg, Wagner, Williams, and Horvath (1995) concluded that

"even the most charitable estimates of the relation between intelligence test scores

and real-world criteria such as job performance indicate that approximately three

fourths of the variance in real-world performance is not accounted for by

Page
number
of quoted
passage.

intelligence test performance" (p. 912). Although Rosenthal (1990) showed, in

another context, that identifying a predictor variable that can account for 25% of

variance is not unimpressive in the human sciences, Sternberg et al.'s (1995) point is

well taken that there are conceptual and psychometric limitations in the traditional

model of intelligence.

After the
first full
citation of
a work with
up to five
authors,
only
the first
author's
surname
followed by
"et al." ("and
others") is
used if
there are
three or
more
authors.

Sternberg's (1985, 1988, 1990) own triarchic theory of intelligence is

emblematic of the view that I characterize in this paper as "multiplex" because it

encompasses the assumption of multiple intelligences, including some that

presumably operate beyond the verbal or mathematical realm (see also Ceci, 1990;

Gardner, 1983). In the remainder of this paper, I will focus on another prominent

Center
headings
(in upper-
case and
lowercase
letters,
and not
italicized)
are used
for major
sections, and
subheadings
(flush left,
in italics)
are used to
subdivide
these major
sections.

example of the multiplex view, the theory of multiple intelligences advanced by

Howard Gardner (1983, 1993b). Gardner has argued against the single general

characteristic assumption and has used the term *intelligences* to embrace multiple

intellectual aptitudes.

Gardner's Theory of Multiple Intelligences

Gardner's Notion of Intelligence

Gardner (1983) described intelligence as encompassing "the ability to solve

problems, or to create products that are valued within one or more cultural settings"

(p. x). In spite of this rather broad definition, he went on to argue that not every real-life skill should be considered under the label of *intelligence*. Rather, he maintained that any talent deemed "intellectual" must fit the following eight criteria:

Numbering the eight criteria sets them off for clarity.

1. The potential must exist to isolate the intelligence by brain damage.

2. Exceptional populations, such as savants, whose members exhibit outstanding but uneven abilities, must provide evidence of the distinctive existence of the particular entity.

3. There must be identifiable core operations--that is, basic information-processing operations that are unique to the particular abilities.

4. There must be a distinctive developmental history--that is, stages through which individuals pass, with individual differences in the ultimate levels of expertise achieved.

5. There should be locatable antecedents (more primitive, less integrated versions) of the intelligence in other species.

6. The intelligence must be open to experimental study, so that predictions of the construct can be subjected to empirical tests.

7. Although no single standardized test can measure the entirety of abilities that are deemed intellectual, standardized tests should provide clues about the intelligence and should predict the performance of some tasks and not others.

8. It must be possible to capture the information content in the intelligence through a symbol system--for example, language or choreographed movements.

Perspectives on Intelligence   8

Seven Kinds of Intelligence

Using these requirements as a base, Gardner argued the importance of studying people within the "normal" range of intelligence, and also of studying those who are gifted or expert in various domains valued by different cultures (see Gardner, 1993a). Gardner further emphasized the importance of studying individuals who have suffered selective brain injuries. Using his list of eight criteria and the research results from four major disciplines (psychology, sociology, anthropology, and biology), Gardner proposed the existence of seven intelligences: (a) logical-mathematical, (b) linguistic, (c) spatial, (d) bodily-kinesthetic, (e) musical, (f) intrapersonal, and (g) interpersonal.

According to Gardner, traditional intelligence, which is language-based and easy to quantify by conventional measures, encompasses *logical-mathematical intelligence* and *linguistic intelligence*. People who are high in logical-mathematical intelligence are identified as skilled in reasoning and computation. People with keen linguistic skills are good with words and language. Gardner maintained, however, that these two kinds of intelligence represent only part of the picture. Thus, he theorized five additional kinds of intelligence.

Spatial intelligence is demonstrated by those who are able to navigate the spatial world with ease. *Bodily-kinesthetic intelligence* is the domain of dancers, athletes, neurosurgeons, and others skilled in carrying and moving their bodies. A person who is *musically intelligent* is talented in discerning themes in music and is sensitive to qualities of melody (e.g., pitch, rhythm, and timbre). The last two intelligences are part of what Gardner termed the "personal intelligences"--that is, the talent to detect various shades of meaning in the emotions, intentions, and behavior of oneself (*intrapersonal intelligence*) and others (*interpersonal intelligence*). Those who are high in intrapersonal intelligence are adept at self-understanding; those who are high in interpersonal intelligence (called *interpersonal acumen* by some others, e.g., Aditya & House, 2002; Rosnow, Skleder, Jaeger, & Rind, 1994) are said to be "people persons" who have a fix on the social and interpersonal landscape.

Independence of Abilities

Crucial to Gardner's formulation of multiple intelligences is the assumption that the various "talents" are not necessarily linked. Someone may perform very poorly in one area (e.g., logical-mathematical) and yet perform well in others (e.g., spatial). This discrepancy calls to mind the stereotype of the brilliant but absentminded scientist, who cannot find the car in the parking lot but can describe in intricate detail the workings of atoms, and perhaps of automobiles. Different intelligences can exist and can presumably be measured quite independently of one another, according to Gardner's formulation. Unfortunately, he argued, because logical-mathematical and linguistic intelligences are valued so highly in American education, tests designed to measure a variety of intelligences still rely heavily on mathematical and verbal skills (Gardner, 1991b, 1993b).

In other words, conventional tests of intelligence measure the same intelligences in slightly different, and perhaps trivial, ways. Therefore, it is not surprising that factor-analytic research (e.g., Spearman, 1927) has often demonstrated a correlation among certain abilities (implying the *g* factor), so that

e.g. for exempli gratia ("for example") is used in parentheses.

individuals who score higher in verbal intelligence tend to score higher than average in reasoning ability. Knowing someone's linguistic intelligence, however, does not necessarily tell us very much about the person's skills with people or music, or in any other realm.

The independence of abilities is also suggested by the fact that while intelligence tests predict school grades reasonably well, they are far less useful in predicting routine successes outside the school setting. Barring low levels of traditional IQ, managerial skills, for example, may be related much more to the ability to manage oneself and the task completion of others, or to the ability to interpret the actions and intentions of others, than to the ability to score high on a standard IQ test or some surrogate measure of academic intelligence (Aditya & House, 2002; Sternberg, 1988). Sternberg (1988, p. 211) called these extracurricular skills "practical intelligence" (and distinguished them from academic intelligence), which in this case seems to be heavily dependent on what Gardner called the personal intelligences.

IQ, although an abbreviation, does not need to be spelled out on first use because it is in Webster's.

Two Main Criticisms of Multiplex Theories

Nontraditional Orientation

Most criticisms of multiplex theories appear to rest on the distinction between intelligence and abilities that have been traditionally characterized as talent (Walters & Gardner, 1986). For example, Ericsson and Charness (1994) argued that expert performance does not usually reflect innate abilities and capacities but is mediated predominantly by physiological adaptations and complex skills. Gardner's (1995) response was that the issue is not whether children are born with innate abilities or capacities, but whether a child who has begun to work in a domain finds a skill and ease in performance that encourage him or her to persevere in the effort. That most people do not usually think of performance skills as "intellectual" is a red herring in this debate, a reflection of the fact that we are still burdened by the traditional idea of intelligence, according to Gardner. Sternberg (1990) reminded us that an individual who has experienced an injury that causes a loss of bodily-kinesthetic ability is not viewed as "mentally retarded." I would add that a person who is very low in social skills, but who scores in the range of normal on IQ tests, is regarded neither as "mentally retarded" nor as "socially retarded."

In short, Gardner's argument is that all the forms of intelligence he proposed may be given equal consideration with the logical-mathematical and linguistic forms so highly valued in Western cultures (Walters & Gardner, 1986). As he put it, "When one revisits the psychological variable that has been most intensively studied, that of psychometric intelligence or g, one finds little evidence to suggest that sheer practice, whether deliberate or not, produces large ultimate differences in performance" (Gardner, 1995, p. 802). Perhaps it is merely because experts have chosen to consider g and the "academic intelligences" more important than the personal intelligences that the term *socially retarded* is not in common use. However, interest in social proclivities appears to be leading to increased attention to the interplay of the personal intelligences and behavior in different situations (Aditya & House, 2002; Rosnow et al., 1994; Sternberg, 1997). In daily life, for example, because some actions and intentions may be intellectually more difficult to read than others, and because interpersonal intelligence can vary greatly in the population, the very nature of this situation can "churn misperceptions into conflicts and conflicts into crises" (Rosnow, 2001, p. 205).

Structure and Amenability to Operationalization and Assessment

Another basic criticism of multiplex theories of intelligence is that, given their amorphous nature, there would seem to be unlimited possibilities of adding to the number of intelligences, beyond even the seven described by Gardner. In fact, since the initial presentation of his theory, Gardner has suggested the possibility of more than seven intelligences and considers the seven to be "working hypotheses" that are fully amenable to revision after further investigation (Walters & Gardner, 1986). Whether this second criticism is reasonable or not depends on one's willingness to regard intelligence as even more inclusive of human talents than it is now.

Also, it has been argued that the standard psychometric approach has the distinct advantage of being more amenable to testing and measurement than is Gardner's theory of multiple intelligences. Gardner, on the other hand, has contended that his seven intelligences are measurable but that conventional tests are inadequate for the job. He has proposed measurements that are more closely linked to what people do in their daily lives--inside and outside academic settings. For example, in applying his theory to education, Gardner (1991a, 1993b) reported assessing children's intelligences by studying their school compositions, choice of activities, performance in athletic events, and other aspects of their behavior and cognitive processes. While this approach is certainly more difficult and complex than the old approach, such measurements are essential from the standpoint of Gardner's theory, and indeed similar progress has been reported by some

Citations
are listed in
alphabet-
ical order
by authors'
surnames.

investigators in replicating the existence of different levels of interpersonal acumen

(Aditya, Buboltz, Darkangelo, & Wilkinson, 2000; Aditya & House, 2002; Rosnow

et al., 1994).

Conclusions

The challenge still remains to develop innovative ways (however complex and

nontraditional) to measure all the different facets of intelligence (Gardner,

Kornhaber, & Wake, 1996; Neisser et al., 1996; Sternberg, 1992). In particular, I

have concentrated on Gardner's theory as one important example of the multiplex

vision of intelligence. This theory encompasses traditional aspects but also attempts

to move our conceptualization of intelligence beyond those boundaries. For

example, when Gardner (1983) described a great dancer as "kinesthetically

intelligent," he alluded to a skill that Spearman would not have accepted as

belonging within the category of intelligence. That Gardner's model is much broader

than the traditional model of intelligence is viewed from some perspectives as a

problem because the broader the theory, the more difficult it is to disconfirm. Based

on my literature search, however, I discerned a trend toward such broad,

interdisciplinary formulations and definitions of intelligence or, as Sternberg (1997)

conceptualized them, whatever mental abilities are necessary to enable persons to

shape and adapt to their environment. With this broader approach, some researchers

are focusing on ways of assessing and improving performance skills that in the past

were ignored or considered far less significant than academic intelligence (e.g.,

Aditya & House, 2002; Gardner, 1991b; Gardner et al., 1996; Sternberg, Torff, &

Grigorenko, 1998).

Perspectives on Intelligence   14

References

Paper presented at a meeting. → Aditya, R. N., Buboltz, W., Darkangelo, D., & Wilkinson, L. (2000, June).

Discriminant validation of a revised interpersonal acumen scale. Paper

presented at the meeting of the American Psychological Society, Miami, FL.

Chapter in an edited book. → Aditya, R. N., & House, R. J. (2002). Interpersonal acumen and leadership across

cultures: Pointers from the GLOBE study. In R. E. Riggio, S. E. Murphy, & F.

J. Pirozzolo (Eds.), *Multiple intelligences and leadership* (pp. 215-240).

Mahwah, NJ: Erlbaum.

Ceci, S. J. (1990). *On intelligence...more or less: A bioecologial treatise on*

intellectual development. Englewood Cliffs, NJ: Prentice Hall.

Ceci, S. J., & Liker, J. (1986). Academic and nonacademic intelligence: An

experimental separation. In R. J. Sternberg & R. Wagner (Eds.), *Practical*

intelligence: Origins of competence in the everyday world (pp. 119-142). New

Article in a journal. → York: Cambridge University Press.

Ericsson, K. A., & Charness, N. (1994). Expert performance: Its structure and

acquisition. *American Psychologist, 49,* 725-747.

Gardner, H. (1983). *Frames of mind: The theory of multiple intelligences.* New

York: Basic Books.

Gardner, H. (1985). *The mind's new science.* New York: Basic Books.

Invert all authors' names (last name, first initial, middle initial). → Gardner, H. (1991a). Assessment in context: The alternative to standardized testing.

In B. R. Gifford & M. C. O'Connor (Eds.), *Changing assessments: Alternative*

views of aptitude, achievement and instruction (pp. 77-119). Boston: Kluwer.

The references begin on a new page.

Page numbers of chapter.

If not a major city in the U.S., list the postal abbreviation of the state.

These editors' names are not inverted.

Perspectives on Intelligence 15

Proper names in titles are capitalized.

Gardner, H. (1991b). *The unschooled mind: How children think and how schools should teach.* New York: Basic Books.

Gardner, H. (1993a). *Creating minds: An anatomy of creativity seen through the lives of Freud, Einstein, Picasso, Stravinsky, Eliot, Graham, and Ghandi.* New York: Basic Books.

Gardner, H. (1993b). *Multiple intelligences: The theory in practice.* New York: Basic Books.

Gardner, H. (1995). Why would anyone become an expert? *American Psychologist, 50,* 802-803.

Gardner, H., Kornhaber, M. L., & Wake, W. K. (1996). *Intelligence: Multiple perspective.* Ft. Worth, TX: Harcourt Brace.

Gilbert, H. B. (1971). Intelligence tests. In L. C. Deighton (Ed.), *The encyclopedia of education* (Vol. 5, pp. 128-135). New York: Macmillan and Free Press.

Guilford, J. P. (1967). *The nature of intelligence.* New York: McGraw-Hill.

Herrnstein, R. J., & Murray, C. (1994). *The bell curve: Intelligence and class structure in American life.* New York: Free Press.

Jensen, A. R. (1969). How much can we boost IQ and scholastic achievement? *Harvard Educational Review, 39,* 1-123.

Levy, J. (1974). Cerebral asymmetries as manifested in split-brain man. In M. Kinsbourne & W. L. Smith (Eds.), *Hemispheric disconnection and cerebral function* (pp. 165-183). Springfield, IL: Charles C Thomas.

Neisser, U., Boodoo, G., Bouchard, T. J., Jr., Boykin, A. W., Brody, N., Ceci, S. J., Halpern, D. F., Loehlin, J. C., Perloff, R., Sternberg, R. J., & Urbina, S.

Two works by the same author in the same year are designated a,b.

Article in an encyclopedia.

Capitalize the first word of the title and the subtitle of a book.

Ampersand (&) before the last authors' name.

Major cities can be listed without a state abbreviation.

Article with eleven authors.

Perspectives on Intelligence   16

(1996). Intelligence: Knowns and unknowns. *American Psychologist, 51,* 77-101.

Reed, T. E., & Jensen, A. R. (1992). Conduction velocity in a brain nerve pathway of normal adult correlates with intelligence. *Intelligence, 16,* 259-272.

Rosenthal, R. (1990). How are we doing in soft psychology? *American Psychologist, 45,* 775-777.

Rosnow, R. L. (2001). Rumor and gossip in interpersonal interaction and beyond: A social exchange perspective. In R. M. Kowalski (Ed.), *Behaving badly: Aversive behaviors in interpersonal relationships* (pp. 203-232). Washington, DC: American Psychological Association.

Rosnow, R. L., Skleder, A. A., Jaeger, M. E., & Rind, B. (1994). Intelligence and the epistemics of interpersonal acumen: Testing some implications of Gardner's theory. *Intelligence, 19,* 93-116.

Siegler, R. S., & Richards, D. D. (1982). The development of intelligence. In R. J. Sternberg (Ed.), *Handbook of human intelligence* (pp. 897-971). New York: Cambridge University Press.

Spearman, C. (1927). *The abilities of man.* New York: Macmillan.

Sternberg, R. J. (1985). *Beyond IQ: A triarchic theory of human intelligence.* New York: Cambridge University Press.

Sternberg, R. J. (1988). *The triarchic mind: A new theory of human intelligence.* New York: Viking.

Sternberg, R. J. (1990). *Metaphors of mind: A new theory of human intelligence.* New York: Cambridge University Press.

"Ed." for one editor.

Article with four authors.

Perspectives on Intelligence   17

Sternberg, R. J. (1992). Ability tests, measurements, and markets. *Journal of Educational Psychology, 84,* 134-140.

Sternberg, R. J. (1997). The concept of intelligence and its role in lifelong learning and success. *American Psychologist, 52,* 1030-1037.

Sternberg, R. J., & Berg, C. A. (1986). Definitions of intelligence: A comparison of the 1921 and 1986 symposia. In R. J. Sternberg & D. K. Detterman (Eds.), *What is intelligence? Contemporary viewpoints on its nature and definition* (pp. 155-162). Norwood, NJ: Ablex.

Sternberg, R. J., Torff, B., & Grigorenko, E. L. (1998). Teaching triarchially improves school achievement. *Journal of Educational Psychology, 90,* 374-384.

Sternberg, R. J., Wagner, R. K., Williams, W. M., & Horvath, J. A. (1995). Testing common sense. *American Psychologist, 50,* 912-927.

Thurstone, L. L. (1938). *Primary mental abilities.* Chicago: University of Chicago Press.

Thurstone, L. L., & Thurstone, T. G. (1941). *Factorial studies of intelligence.* (Psychometric Society Psychometric Monographs No. 2). Chicago: University of Chicago Press.

Walters, J. M., & Gardner, H. (1986). The theory of multiple intelligences: Some issues and answers. In R. J. Sternberg & R. K. Wagner (Eds.), *Practical intelligence: Nature and origins of competence in the everyday world* (pp. 163-181). New York: Cambridge University Press.

Italicize the volume number of a journal, but not the page numbers of the article.

Serial work.

Serial number.

"Eds." for two editors.

B

SAMPLE RESEARCH REPORT

Pages are numbered consecutively, beginning with the title page, and contain a short heading of two or three words from the title.

Restaurant Tipping   1

The title is double-spaced in uppercase and lowercase letters and centered between the left and right margins.

Effect of an After-Meal Candy on Restaurant Tipping:

An Experimental Study in a Naturalistic Setting

The student's name is centered, two double-spaced lines below the title.

Jane Doe

Psychology 333

Instructor: Prof. Bruce Rind

(Date the Research Report is Submitted)

The course number, the instructor's name, and the date the paper is submitted are double-spaced.

*The abstract
begins on a
new page.*

*The abstract
is not
indented.*

Abstract

Previous research has shown that waiters and waitresses (i.e., servers) can increase their tips by using a variety of techniques that generally involve creating an impression of friendliness. This study examined another technique that was hypothesized to enhance customers' favorable impressions of the server and, in turn, increase the size of the tip. The server in this study was provided with a basket of miniature chocolate candies, which she was instructed to bring with her when presenting the check in three experimental conditions. In the "1-piece condition," the server offered each customer in the dining party one candy of his or her choice. In the "2-piece condition," the server offered each person two candies, on the premise that this gesture would further underscore the server's friendliness. In the "1 + 1 condition," she offered one candy and said, "Oh, have another piece"; this procedure was intended to emphasize not only her friendliness but also her personal generosity (consistent with reciprocity theory). In the control condition, the server presented the check without any candy offer. Although the tip percentage in the control condition differed significantly only from that in the 2-piece and 1 + 1 conditions, there was, as hypothesized, increased tipping from control group to 1-piece to 2-piece to 1 + 1 condition; the linear contrast was statistically significant and the effect size substantial. Statistical power considerations and ideas for further investigation are discussed.

*For
conciseness,
digits are
used for all
numbers in
the abstract,
except those
that begin
a sentence.*

*Briefly, the abstract
tells why the research
was done, what was
hypothesized, what
the results were, and
what else appears in
the discussion section.*

*Use a
12-point
typeface,
preferably
Times New
Roman or
Courier.*

The text
begins
on a new
page and
opens with
a repetition
of the title.

The first line
of every
paragraph
in the text
is indented
five to seven
spaces.

Restaurant Tipping   3

Effect of an After-Meal Candy on Restaurant Tipping:

An Experimental Study in a Naturalistic Setting

More than 1 million people in the United States work as waiters or waitresses

The
opening
paragraph
sets the
stage in
an inviting
way and
explains the
importance
of the
research.

who serve in restaurants (Department of Commerce, 1990, p. 391). Although they

are generally paid for their service by their employers, the major source of income

for servers is usually tips from customers (Lynn & Mynier, 1993; Schmidt, 1985).

Because tips are so important to the livelihood of most servers, knowledge about

factors that affect customers' tipping behavior is valuable. Recently, a growing

number of studies have examined factors hypothesized to affect tipping. This

research has shown that servers can increase their tipping percentages by a variety

of techniques (Lynn, 1996).

An
ampersand
(&) appears
in
parentheses
where "and"
is used
otherwise.

Although
the left
margin
is even,
the right
margin
is ragged.

Some of these techniques involve direct interpersonal action on the part of the

server, such as touching or smiling at the customer. For example, Hornik (1992) had

three waitresses at two restaurants either not touch their customers, touch them for

The
statistical
symbol
for a
percentage
(%) is used
only when
it is
preceded
by a
number.

half a second on the shoulder, or touch them twice on the palm of the hand for half a

second each time. Tips increased from 12% to 14% to 17% in the three conditions,

respectively. Tidd and Lockard (1978) had a waitress give customers sitting alone a

large, open-mouth smile or a small, closed-mouth smile. Customers in the former

condition tipped on average 48 cents compared to 20 cents in the latter condition. In

a similar vein, Lynn and Mynier (1993) instructed servers either to squat to the eye

level of their customers or stand erect during the initial visit to the table; the

squatting increased tips. Garrity and Degelman (1990) reported that a server earned

Citations
buttress
the
introduc-
tion.

On all four sides,
leave a margin
of at least one inch
for the reader's
comments.

Restaurant Tipping   4

higher tips when introducing herself by her first name during her initial visit (23%

average tip) than when she did not introduce herself (15% average tip).

Other effective techniques employed an indirect stimulus to encourage tipping.

Double quotation marks here are because "thank you" is the verbatim expression that was used.

Rind and Bordia (1996) had servers either draw or not draw a happy face on the

backs of customers' checks before delivering them. The happy face increased tips

for the female server but did not increase tips for the male server (for whom this

practice may have been regarded as "gender-inappropriate" by customers). Rind and

Bordia (1995) also found that writing "thank you" on the backs of checks resulted in

an increase in tips from 16% to 18%. Finally, McCall and Belmont (1995) had

servers present checks either on a tray with credit card emblems on it or on a tray

with no emblems and found that tipping percentages were higher in the former

condition.

Note the orderly presentation of ideas, which tells the instructor that the student has a clear understanding of the project.

These techniques, except for the last one, have in common that the servers

were doing something that might increase the customers' impressions of

friendliness. Another such technique was experimentally examined in the present

study. When presenting the check to the dining party, the server sometimes also

presented a gift of assorted candies. Three hypotheses were evaluated. First, on the

assumption that the gift would be perceived by customers as a gesture of

friendliness, it was predicted that the presentation of the gift would have the effect

of stimulating tipping, in comparison with a no-gift control group. On the

assumption that this effect is cumulative (i.e., up to a certain point), the second

hypothesis was that an offer of more candies would stimulate tipping even more.

The third hypothesis was that when customers were under the impression that the

The introduction concludes with your hypotheses or predictions.

Abbreviation for id est ("that is").

offer of a gift also reflected the server's generosity (i.e., as opposed to the

restaurant's protocol), there would be a further increase in tipping. This third

hypothesis was derived from research on reciprocity, which found that individuals

felt especially obligated to return a favor to the person responsible for the favor

(Regan, 1971).

First-level headings are centered.

Method

Second-level headings are flush left and in italics (or underlined).

Participants

Eighty dining parties eating dinner at an upscale Italian-American restaurant

located in central New Jersey served as participants. The total number of customers

in the dining parties was 293, with a mean of 3.67 customers per dining party ($SD =$

1.97). The size of the dining parties ranged from 2 to 12.

Procedure

A female server, who also served as the experimental accomplice, was

provided with a small wicker basket that was filled with Hershey Assorted Miniature

chocolates. The candies were of four types: (a) dark chocolate bars, (b) milk

chocolate bars, (c) rice and chocolate bars, and (d) peanut butter and chocolate bars.

The server was also given a stack of index cards, each of which contained an

instruction telling her to do one of four things when presenting the check. In the

control condition, she was instructed to present the check as usual without any

candy offer. In the three experimental conditions, she was instructed to bring along

the basket of candy when presenting the check.

In one experimental condition, the server was instructed to offer each customer

in the dining party one piece of candy of his or her choice (the "1-piece condition").

Margin annotations:

The method section, like all the major sections of the text, follow each other without a page break.

Statistical symbol for the standard deviation is in italics.

The list is lettered for clarity.

Double quotation marks are used here to indicate that the term is an invented expression, but quotation marks are not used again when the expression is repeated later.

In a second experimental condition, she was instructed to offer each customer in the party two pieces of candy (the "2-piece condition"). In the third experimental condition, she was instructed to offer one candy and say, "Oh, have another piece," as if the offer of a second piece were a generous afterthought (the "1+1 condition"); this treatment was intended to emphasize to customers the server's (as opposed to the restaurant's) generosity.

Double quotation marks here because this was the verbatim statement by the server.

The cards were thoroughly shuffled to ensure that the order of the four types of instructions was random. When it was time to present the check, the server reached into her apron pocket and randomly chose a card. The server was instructed to thank the dining party after their selection of candies, and then to leave the table immediately to avoid any nonessential interaction with the party. After the dining party had left the restaurant, the server recorded (on the same card used to determine the dining party's treatment condition) the amount of the tip left by the party, the amount of the bill before taxes, and the party size.

Past tense is used here for the results; it is also proper to use the present tense to discuss the results.

Results

Before turning to the data analysis, I consulted with the instructor regarding two possible approaches illustrated in the textbook used in this course (Rosnow & Rosenthal, 2002). One approach consisted of comparing the control group with each of the other groups by using either independent *t* tests or, to control for heterogeneity of variance in some comparisons, a more complicated procedure known as *Satterthwaite's method,* which would adjust the degrees of freedom of a modified *t* test. The second approach consisted of a one-way analysis of variance (ANOVA) on all four groups, then used the mean square error (*MSE*) of this

The results section follows the method section without a page break.

Abbreviations are usually first spelled out, unless they are assumed to be universally understood.

Statistical symbol for the analysis of variance is not in italics.

ANOVA as the pooled error term of three *t* tests and carved a linear contrast out of

the ANOVA's sum of squares between groups. After discussion with the instructor, I

chose the second approach because it enabled me to maximize the degrees of

freedom of the *t* tests as well as perform a single contrast to evaluate the

hypothesized monotonic increase in tipping. A handheld scientific calculator was

used for all calculations; the scores and calculations are shown in the appendix at the

end of this report.

> Subgroups are denoted by lowercase n in italics.

   The dependent measure was defined as the tip percentage--that is, the tip

amount divided by the bill amount before taxes, which was then multiplied by 100.

Descriptive results are given in Table 1, which shows average tip percentages in the

four conditions, computed as the arithmetic mean (*M*) of $n = 20$ percentage scores in

each condition. The one-way analysis of variance (ANOVA) on these results was

highly significant, with $F(3, 76) = 15.51$, $p = .000000058$. Three *t* tests that focused

> Degrees of freedom are 3 for the numerator and 76 for the denominator of this F statistic.

on the specific hypotheses were optimized by use of the mean square error (*MSE* =

4.45) and denominator degrees of freedom (*df* = 76) of the overall ANOVA.

   The first prediction was that tipping would be greater in the 1-piece condition

than in the control condition. Although Table 1 shows the direction of means to be

consistent with this prediction, the *t* test comparing these two conditions was not

significant, with $t(76) = .95$, $p = .17$ one-tailed. The corresponding effect size,

calculated directly from the *t* statistic, was small ($r_{\text{effect size}} = .15$). Furthermore, the

95% confidence interval ranged from -.17 to .44, which left open the possibility of a

small effect in the opposite direction.

> Degrees of freedom are 76 for this t test, and the p value is denoted as one-tailed. If it were two-tailed, this p value would be .34 (i.e., .17 x 2).

> Many statisticians report the actual descriptive level of significance because it is more precise than "$p < .01$," but the APA manual encourages limiting the number of decimal places of all statistical values to two. Check with your instructor to find out whether a particular approach is preferred in your course.

Restaurant Tipping   8

On the assumption that the effect of the server's gift giving on subsequent

tipping would be cumulative, the second prediction was that tipping would be still

greater in the 2-piece condition. The means in Table 1 are again consistent with the

hypothesis, and in this case, the difference between the control and the 2-piece

condition mean was highly significant, with $t(76) = 3.99$, $p = .000075$ one-tailed.

Further, the effect size computed from this t was large ($r_{effect\ size} = .54$), and the

95% confidence interval was reassuring because it revealed the lower limit of the

effect size range to be in the predicted direction and of moderate size ($r_{effect\ size}$

ranged from .28 to .73).

The third prediction, which was derived from reciprocity research, was that

creating the impression that the server was generous (the 1 + 1 condition) would

result in a further increase in tipping. The t test comparing the 1 + 1 and control

conditions was highly significant, and the effect size was very large, with $t(76) =$

6.05, $p = .000000025$ one-tailed, $r_{effect\ size} = .70$. The 95% confidence interval

ranged from $r_{effect\ size} = .50$ to .83.

Finally, to provide a focused evaluation of the increase in tipping from control

to 1-piece to 2-piece to 1 + 1 conditions, a linear contrast was computed by means

of a procedure shown in the textbook (Rosnow & Rosenthal, 2002, pp. 403-406). In

a contrast analysis, the prediction of interest is represented by fixed weights (called

lambda weights) that must sum to zero. I chose lambda weights of -3, -1, +1, +3 to

represent the control, 1-piece, 2-piece, and 1 + 1 conditions, respectively. The

results of this analysis are summarized in Table 2, which indicates that the linear

contrast was highly significant, with $F(1, 76) = 44.97$, $p = .0000000031$, and the

Symbol for correlation (r) is in italics, but the subscript is not.

effect size large ($r = .61$); the 95% confidence interval ranged from $r_{\text{effect size}} = .45$ to .73.

The discussion follows the results section without a page break.

Discussion

The discussion begins with a statement of the predictions and the results.

It was hypothesized that offering a favor in the form of chocolate candies would stimulate tipping, and that the more candy offered, the greater would be the tip, with the largest tip percentage predicted in the condition in which the server was also meant to be perceived as personally responsible for the gift. Although the observed condition means were consistent with the three hypotheses, and the linear contrast was consistent with the hypothesized monotonic increase in tipping, the t test comparing the control and 1-piece conditions was not statistically significant.

In this course, we have been taught to pay heed to statistical power considerations before embracing the conclusion of "no effect" just because the null hypothesis has not been rejected. I did not do a power analysis, but my inspection of the power table in the textbook, which lists the total Ns required to detect different effect sizes at .05 two-tailed, leads me to believe that the power of my t test comparing the control and 1-piece conditions was substantially lower than the recommended level of .80, even though I used a one-tailed test. However, even had I been able to anticipate the need for more dining parties in the case of the comparison between the control and 1-piece conditions, I was pretty much limited to a total N of 80 because of time constraints.

The APA manual emphasizes the importance of statistical power as an issue in null hypothesis significance testing, particularly when negative results are reported.

Clearly, further research is needed to replicate the relationships in this investigation, in which case it should be possible to improve statistical power by

The discussion concludes by noting the limitations of the study and ideas for further investigation.

using a meta-analytic procedure to obtain an overall probability value (Rosnow &

Rosenthal, 2002). Research is also needed on the separate and interacting roles of

reciprocity and perceptions of friendliness. There is also a need to verify the roles of

"friendliness" and "generosity" presumed by my hypotheses. Finally, additional

research is needed to examine the generalizability of the current findings to male

servers and other female servers, other types of restaurants (e.g., midscale), other

regions of the country, and other types of gifts.

The references begin
on a new page.

Restaurant Tipping   11

References

Publication
in which
the author
is also the
publisher.

Capitalize
proper
nouns
in the
title.

American Psychological Association. (2001). *Publication manual of the American*

Psychological Association (5th ed.). Washington, DC: Author.

Government
report.

Department of Commerce. (1990). *Statistical abstracts of the United States.*

Washington, DC: Author.

Journal
article with
two authors.

Garrity, K., & Degelman, D. (1990). Effect of server introduction on restaurant

tipping. *Journal of Applied Social Psychology, 20,* 168-172.

Hornik, J. (1992). Tactile stimulation and consumer response. *Journal of Consumer*

Research, 19, 449-458.

Journal
titles and
volume
numbers
are in
italics.

One-author
entries
precede
multiple-
author
entries
beginning
with the
same
surname.

Lynn, M. (1996). Seven ways to increase servers' tips. *Cornell Hotel and Restaurant*

Administration Quarterly, 37(3), 24-29.

Lynn, M., & Mynier, K. (1993). Effect of server posture on restaurant tipping.

Journal of Applied Social Psychology, 23, 678-685.

McCall, M., & Belmont, H. J. (1995). *Credit card insignia and tipping: Evidence for*

an associative link. Unpublished manuscript, Ithaca College.

Capitalize
the first
word of
the title
and the
subtitle.

Unpublished
manuscript.

Regan, D. T. (1971). Effects of a favor and liking on compliance. *Journal of*

Experimental Social Psychology, 7, 627-639.

Rind, B., & Bordia, P. (1995). Effect of server's "thank you" and personalization on

References
with the
same
authors in
the same
order are
arranged
by year of
publication.

restaurant tipping. *Journal of Applied Social Psychology, 25,* 745-751.

Rind, B., & Bordia, P. (1996). Effect of restaurant tipping of male and female

servers drawing a happy, smiling face on the backs of customers' checks.

Journal of Applied Social Psychology, 26, 218-225.

References are double-spaced
in a hanging-indent format.
If this is difficult to do, the
APA style permits you to
indent your references with
five-to-seven-space paragraph
indents.

Restaurant Tipping   12

Book in
a fourth
edition. →

Rosnow, R. L., & Rosenthal, R. (2002). *Beginning behavioral research: A*

   conceptual primer (4th ed.). Upper Saddle River, NJ: Prentice Hall.

Schmidt, D. G. (1985). Tips: The mainstay of hotel workers' pay. *Monthly Labor*

   Review, 108, 50-61.

Tidd, K., & Lockard, J. (1978). Monetary significance of the affiliative smile: A case

   for reciprocal altruism. *Bulletin of the Psychometric Society, 11,* 344-346.

Table
number
and title
(which is in
italics) are
flush left.

Restaurant Tipping   13

Table 1

Mean Tip Percentage, Standard Deviation, and Sample Size

Row and
column
headings
are
telegraphic.

		Treatment condition		
Results	No candy	1 piece	2 pieces	1+1 pieces
M	18.95	19.59	21.62	22.99
SD	1.46	1.71	2.45	2.43
n	20	20	20	20

Where
means are
reported, an
associated
measure of
variability
is also
reported.

Note. The mean (*M*) value denotes the average tip percentage in the particular condition; I calculated the tip percentage for each dining party by dividing the tip amount by the bill amount before taxes, and then multiplying by 100. The standard deviation (*SD*) refers to the variability of *n* = 20 tip percentages around the mean value.

The word
Note is
italicized
and
followed
by a period.

Table notes
are placed
below the
table, and
in this case,
the note
clearly
explains
what
appears in
the table.

Tables are placed
after the references,
each table on its
own separate page.

Because the linear contrast and noncontrast sums of squares were carved out of the between-groups sum of squares, the carved-out sources are slightly indented to represent this fact.

Table 2 begins on a new page.

Restaurant Tipping   14

Table 2

Analysis of Variance With Linear Contrast

Source	SS	df	MS	F	r
Between groups	207.06	3	69.02	15.51[†]	--
Linear contrast	200.12	1	200.12	44.97[†]	.61
Noncontrast	6.94	2	3.47	0.78	--
Within error	338.22	76	(4.45)		

The APA style is to round values to two decimal places to make the values read more easily in tables that contain a lot of information.

The mean square error (MSE) is enclosed in parentheses.

Note. The value enclosed in parentheses represents mean square error. No effect size indicator is represented for the two F tests with numerator $df > 1$, as "multiple degree-of-freedom indicators tend to be less useful than effect indicators that decompose multiple degree-of-freedom tests into meaningful one degree-of-freedom effects" (American Psychological Association, 2001, p. 26).

The page number of the quoted statement is indicated.

[†]$p < .0001$.

The APA style is to use asterisks (*) to identify two-tailed probability values and an alternate symbol (e.g., daggers) for one-tailed p values. Because it is characteristic of F distributions that the p values are naturally one-tailed, a dagger is used to represent the p value in this table.

The appendix begins on a new page and is the final section of the report.

Appendix

no candy	1-piece	2-piece	1+1 condition
18.92	18.87	22.78	17.38
18.43	20.49	15.81	23.38
18.67	17.54	19.16	25.05
18.27	19.35	19.01	21.83
18.92	20.65	21.60	24.43
17.84	19.17	18.45	21.11
19.57	19.73	23.41	25.09
19.12	17.88	21.37	24.35
18.67	21.00	22.01	25.37
22.94	22.33	20.65	21.87
19.26	19.75	20.92	23.87
19.49	20.79	26.17	22.62
19.12	20.52	23.31	26.73
15.90	22.66	23.85	21.81
19.29	18.60	22.30	23.60
19.12	18.60	21.34	23.06
21.70	20.07	18.89	24.05
16.72	14.64	23.47	16.72
17.75	19.01	25.69	22.43
19.35	20.08	22.12	25.08

M	18.9525	19.5865	21.6155	22.9915	20.7865
S	1.4948	1.7525	2.5092	2.4898	
σ	1.4570	1.7081	2.4457	2.4268	

It is not necessary to type the appendix, but it is important to provide the instructor with the raw data and sufficient details to explain how you computed the results, if you did so on a handheld calculator.

$SS_{between} = \sum [n_k (M_k - M_G)^2]$

$= 20(18.9525 - 20.7865)^2 + 20(19.5865 - 20.7865)^2$
$\quad + 20(21.6155 - 20.7865)^2 + 20(22.9915 - 20.7865)^2$

$= 207.0564$

$S^2_{pooled} = [(1.4948)^2 + (1.7525)^2 + (2.5092)^2 + (2.4898)^2] / 4$

$= 4.4502$

Restaurant Tipping   16

$$F(3,76) = \frac{SS_{between}/K-1}{S^2_{pooled}} = \frac{207.0564/3}{4.4502} = 15.5091$$

$$p = 5.8E-8$$

$$t = \frac{M_1 - M_2}{\sqrt{(\frac{1}{n_1} + \frac{1}{n_2})S^2_{pooled}}} \quad \text{with } df = N-K = 80-4 = 76$$

$$\text{and } r_{effect\ size} = \sqrt{\frac{t^2}{t^2 + df}}, \text{ where } df = n_1 + n_2 - 2 = 38$$

1-piece vs. control

$$t = \frac{19.5865 - 18.9565}{\sqrt{(\frac{1}{20} + \frac{1}{20})4.4502}} = 0.9504 \quad p = .173 \text{ one-tailed}$$

$$r = \sqrt{\frac{(.9504)^2}{(.9504)^2 + 38}} = .1524 \quad (95\% = -.17 \text{ to } .44)$$

2-piece vs. control

$$t = \frac{21.6155 - 18.9565}{\sqrt{(\frac{1}{20} + \frac{1}{20})4.4502}} = 3.9919 \quad p = 7.5E-5$$

$$r = \sqrt{\frac{(3.9919)^2}{(3.9919)^2 + 38}} = .5436 \quad (95\% = .28 \text{ to } .73)$$

1+1 condition vs. control

$$t = \frac{22.9915 - 18.9565}{\sqrt{(\frac{1}{20} + \frac{1}{20})4.4502}} = 6.0546 \quad p = 2.5E-8$$

$$r = \sqrt{\frac{(6.0546)^2}{(6.0546)^2 + 38}} = .7007 \quad (95\% = .50 \text{ to } .83)$$

The results, although rounded to two decimal places in the text (as stipulated by the APA manual) are not rounded in the calculations.

Linear contrast weights = $-3, -1, +1, +3$

$r_{alerting} = r_{M\lambda} = .9831$

$r^2_{alerting} = (.9831)^2 = .9665$

$SS_{linear} = MS_{linear} = 207.0564 \times .9665 = 200.1200$

$$F_{contrast}(1, 76) = \frac{200.1200}{4.4502} = 44.9688 \quad p = 3.1 E-9$$

$SS_{noncontrast} = 207.0564 - 200.1200 = 6.9364$

$MS_{noncontrast} = \frac{6.9364}{2} = 3.4682$

$$F_{noncontrast}(2, 76) = \frac{3.4682}{4.4502} = 0.7793 \quad p = .46$$

$$r_{effect size} = \sqrt{\frac{F_{contrast}}{F_{contrast} + F_{noncontrast}(df_{noncontrast}) + df_{within}}}$$

$$= \sqrt{\frac{44.9688}{44.9688 + 0.7793(2) + 76}} = .6058$$

$95\% CI = .45 \ to \ .73$

The calculations are reported in a way that walks the reader through the logical sequence used, clearly explaining how the summary results in the research report were obtained.

Index

TO THE OWNER OF THIS BOOK:

We hope that you have found *Writing Papers in Psychology, Sixth Edition,* useful. So that this book can be improved in a future edition, would you take the time to complete this sheet and return it? Thank you.

School and address: _____

Department: _____

Instructor's name: _____

1. What I like most about this book is: _____

_____

_____

2. What I like least about this book is: _____

_____

_____

3. My general reaction to this book is: _____

_____

4. The name of the course in which I used this book is: _____

_____

5. Were all of the chapters of the book assigned for you to read? _____

   If not, which ones weren't? _____

6. In the space below, or on a separate sheet of paper, please write specific suggestions for improving this book and anything else you'd care to share about your experience in using the book.

_____

_____

_____

_____

_____

Optional:

Your name: _____ Date: _____

May Brooks/Cole quote you, either in promotion for *Writing Papers in Psychology, Sixth Edition* or in future publishing ventures?

Yes: _____ No: _____

Sincerely,

Ralph and Mimi Rosnow